"Ever the engaging and warm-hearted scholar, author Robert Velarde
manages to instruct us in the details of Lewis's life and thought
while also keeping us thoroughly entertained.
A delightful journey in the company of the most congenial of companions."

JIM WARE, author of *God of the Fairy Tale* and *Finding God in The Hobbit*,
and coauthor of *Finding God in the Lord of the Rings, Finding God in the Land of Narnia*
and *Shedding Light on His Dark Materials*

"An engaging and imaginative fantasy journey through C. S. Lewis's life and thought
that nicely blends two very different kinds of story lines:
biographical vignettes and theological arguments. The result is a kind of mix
of *The Great Divorce, It's a Wonderful Life* and *A Christmas Carol.*
This book should be made into a movie."

PETER KREEFT, professor of philosophy, Boston College, and
author of *C. S. Lewis for the Third Millennium* and *Between Heaven and Hell*

"Robert Velarde has pulled off a rare and wonderful feat:
a book that is at once enjoyable, edifying, erudite
and apologetically engaging. Bravo!"

DOUGLAS GROOTHUIS, professor of philosophy, Denver Seminary

"Robert Velarde brings amazingly fresh creativity to this work based on
the writings of C. S. Lewis. Velarde exhibits extensive knowledge of
Lewis's canon and brings fresh insights about his work.
Whether one is a veteran reader or is new to Lewis, Robert Velarde's
Conversations with C. S. Lewis will stoke a fire of interest
in the works of this beloved author."

ALEX MCFARLAND, president, Southern Evangelical Seminary

"C. S. Lewis, imagining what the resurrection might be like, once wrote to his fictitious correspondent Malcolm, 'I can now communicate to you the fields of my boyhood—they are building-estates to-day—only imperfectly, by words. Perhaps the day is coming when I can take you for a walk through them' (*Letters to Malcolm: Chiefly on Prayer*, Letter XXII). In *Conversations with C. S. Lewis*, Robert Velarde takes us on just such an imaginative journey with C. S. Lewis, not only to the fields of Lewis's boyhood but throughout the major scenes of Lewis's unparalleled life. What C. S. Lewis fan hasn't longed, and dreamed of what it would be like, to actually sit down with Lewis and ask him questions about his life and thought? With this book Velarde momentarily quenches a thirst which most Lewis fans thought only a heavenly Lewisian conversation would ever satisfy.

"However, that is not all. *Conversations with C. S. Lewis* is a creative apologetic unequaled since Peter Kreeft's *Between Heaven and Hell* was first published. This is a book eminently suitable for passing on to one's atheist, agnostic and seeking friends. If one wants to become acquainted with the basic outline of Lewis's life and thought or if one desires to explore in an entertaining fashion the greatest philosophical and theological questions of all time, reading *Conversations with C. S. Lewis* by Robert Velarde is an excellent place to start. However, let the reader beware: once you pick up this book and begin to read you won't want to put it down until you have walked with C. S. Lewis to the surprising end of this fascinating journey."

WILL VAUS, author of *Mere Theology: A Guide to the Thought of C. S. Lewis*

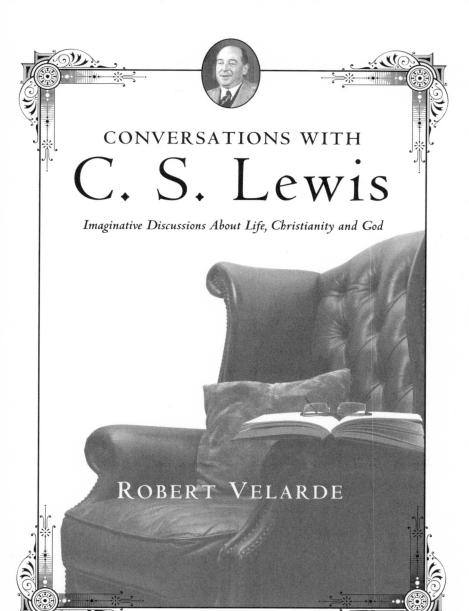

CONVERSATIONS WITH

C. S. Lewis

Imaginative Discussions About Life, Christianity and God

ROBERT VELARDE

IVP Books

An imprint of InterVarsity Press
Downers Grove, Illinois

InterVarsity Press
P.O. Box 1400, Downers Grove, IL 60515-1426
World Wide Web: www.ivpress.com
E-mail: email@ivpress.com

InterVarsity Press® *is the book-publishing division of InterVarsity Christian Fellowship/USA*®*, a student movement active on campus at hundreds of universities, colleges and schools of nursing in the United States of America, and a member movement of the International Fellowship of Evangelical Students. For information about local and regional activities, write Public Relations Dept., InterVarsity Christian Fellowship/ USA, 6400 Schroeder Rd., P.O. Box 7895, Madison, WI 53707-7895, or visit the IVCF website at <www.intervarsity.org>.*

Scripture quotations, unless otherwise noted, are from the King James Version of the Bible.

Conversations with C. S. Lewis *is a work of fiction. Names, characters, places and incidents are either the product of the author's imagination or, if real, are used fictitiously.*

Design: Cindy Kiple
Images: background: Brendon De Suza/iStockphoto
      C. S. Lewis: Martin Poole/Getty Images
      spectacles on book: Stephen Toner/Getty Images

ISBN 978-0-8308-3483-9

Printed in the United States of America ∞

Library of Congress Cataloging-in-Publication Data

Velarde, Robert, 1969-
   Conversations with C. S. Lewis: imaginative discussions about life,
   Christianity, and God/Robert Velarde.
      p. cm.
   Includes bibliographical references (p.) and index.
   ISBN 978-0-8308-3483-9 (pbk.: alk. paper)
   1. Lewis, C. S. (Clive Staples), 1898-1963. 2. Theology. 3.
   Christianity. 4. Apologetics. I. Title.
   BX4827.L44V45 2008
   230.092—dc22

                                 2008002818

P	19	18	17	16	15	14	13	12	11	10	9	8	7	6	5	4	3	2
Y	24	23	22	21	20	19	18	17	16	15	14	13	12	11	10	09	08	

For Anthony, Vincent, Dante and Marcus

"Sons are a heritage from the LORD,
children a reward from him."

PSALM 127:3 (NIV)

Contents

〜 I 〜

Surprised by C. S. Lewis

In which I meet a strange man claiming to be C. S. Lewis and our journey begins.

C. S. Lewis died in 1963, but I met him last week. At least, I think I did. He appeared in my hospital room, sitting quietly in a worn but plush vinyl chair, working on a crossword puzzle in a tattered newspaper. The man must have come in while I slept. I remember opening my eyes, rubbing them to clear away the blur of my dreams and suddenly realizing I was not alone.

"Hello?" My voice, tired and dry, sounded hoarse and soft. The man ignored me, so I reached for a glass of water and took a drink in order to clear my throat, then spoke louder. "Hello?"

"Good evening, young man." The man's deep voice and distinctly British accent stirred me further into wakefulness. At thirty-three I did not consider myself a "young man," but, compared to the stranger, it made some sense.

The man carefully folded the newspaper and tucked it into a coat pocket. He removed his reading glasses and put them in another pocket.

He looked to be in his late fifties or perhaps early sixties. Although he had some dark hair left, mainly on the sides, he was mostly bald. His skin had a florid appearance, while his clothing made him look disheveled.

The brown jacket he wore appeared as though it had been pulled from beneath a pile of laundry; its wrinkles were visible even across the room. He wore dark corduroy pants that looked no better than his coat, but his kind expression put me at ease, despite my reservations about this unexpected intruder.

"Visiting hours are over," I said. "Besides, I think you have the wrong room."

Ignoring my comments, he glanced at the windows.

"I see it is snowing," he said. It was an understatement—we were having a blizzard. "I always liked snow, but it can't go on forever. Now then," he continued, turning his attention back to me, "what is that you are reading?" I glanced over to my right at the paperback on the food tray.

Slightly embarrassed, I replied, "*Mere Christianity* by C. S. Lewis. Are you familiar with it?"

"I dare say I am!" He chuckled. "In fact, I wrote it. Well, actually I first spoke most of it on the radio, then later polished it up a bit for print."

I quickly looked for the call button to summon a nurse. Clearly I was in the presence of a lunatic, or at least a liar. The button was on a cord, though, which had fallen to the floor. Since there did not appear to be any immediate danger, I decided to chat with this eccentric man for a bit. It would, I reasoned, make for a nice diversion other than television. Besides, considering the seriousness of my condition, I was eager to take my mind off things.

"You wrote it?" I said cautiously. "But C. S. Lewis wrote it and he's . . . well, he's dead."

"Yes, I know. But surely you don't think death means ceasing to exist?"

"Actually, I do."

"I see. I'll make a note to discuss that with you later. Nevertheless, I wrote that book. Where did you get it, by the way?"

"It was a gift from . . . someone I used to be close to. But, Mr., uh, Lewis," I said, deciding to play along for the moment.

"Call me Jack."

"Excuse me? I thought you said you were C. S. Lewis."

I reached over to the book and began reading the short biography on the back. "Clive Staples Lewis (1898-1963) was professor of medieval and renaissance literature at Cambridge University . . ."

"Oh, yes, I know all about that. Still, if you had a name like Clive Staples, wouldn't you rather people call you Jack?" He said this with a certain amount of seriousness, yet his eyes were sparkling, as if with a hidden, or perhaps not so hidden, delight and playfulness. "My friends call me Jack, and you may call me Jack as well."

"All right, Jack. My name is Clerk—Thomas Clerk. But you can call me Tom."

"Very well, Tom. Let us move on to other issues, shall we? You are familiar with *A Christmas Carol* by Dickens?"

"Yes, I've seen the movie."

"A cinema? Oh my, you really do need some work. Read the book sometime. I think you will find it more stimulating. At any rate, you do recall that Scrooge is visited by three spirits in the story?" He looked up, thoughtfully. "Well, four if one counts Marley, I suppose."

"Yes, I know the story. The spirits of Christmas past, present and future visit him, right? But I don't believe in the supernatural."

"Then let me add that to the growing list of topics we need to cover. At any rate, for lack of a better word, you could say that I am a spirit, though that word doesn't really suit me."

Now I began to wish that I could reach the call button and summon a nurse. Maybe this man had escaped from the mental health ward. Still, he didn't seem particularly dangerous.

"So, Mr. Lewis—"

"Jack, if you please."

"So, Jack, what you are saying is that you are C. S. Lewis and somehow your presence here is similar to the presence of the spirits in *A Christmas Carol.*" It sounded ridiculous. Was I being set up? Maybe a practical joke?

"Yes, that about sums it up, Tom. However, I am not here to show you your life, but mine."

"I don't understand."

"Over the course of the next several hours," said the man, "we will travel together to a number of places of significance in my life. It is my hope that we will cover a lot of ground including theology, philosophy, literature, morality and so forth. You will even meet some friends of mine along the way—both real and imaginary."

Who was this confident stranger? He seemed nice enough, but no doubt he must be mentally unstable. I began to suspect that I was dreaming, but it was certainly unlike any dream I'd ever had. Perhaps my chemo treatments had broken down my ability to think clearly.

"What do you mean by 'both real and imaginary'?" I asked.

"Simply that you will meet people in my life who really lived, as well as people and creatures that I made up for some of my stories. You know, in addition to that book you have there, I also wrote a number of works of creative fiction." He did not come across as proud, but as merely and plainly factual.

"You mean like *The Screwtape Letters?*"

"You've read it?" The man smiled.

"Well, no," I answered, feeling foolish, "but it's mentioned in this biography." I gestured to the paperback, which I had set back on the table.

"So you plan to introduce me to imaginary characters?" I asked.

"Real and imaginary, yes—though I don't know that you will find it pleasant to meet a devil like Screwtape or even his nephew, Wormwood. When we get to that part, perhaps we can start with the Narnia stories, though I must warn you that not all the imaginary creatures of that world are pleasant either."

"Okay," I began slowly, still trying to make some sense out of the situation, "but why meet these people? Why not just stay here and have our discussions? I'm not really in a condition to travel, and my hospital gown leaves something to be desired."

"Your condition won't be a problem. As to why we can't just stay here and have our discussions, I think it wise to meet the people who, for better or for worse, shaped important parts of my life and character," replied the man. "You will find that your journey, though no doubt different from mine in key respects, has one important thing in common with mine."

"What is that?"

"History," he said. "History and the people in it. We are in many respects shaped by our times and by those who influence our lives, as well as those we in turn influence. In the end, Tom, it is you who will decide your fate, but my advice is that you realize you are not alone."

"Assuming I agree to travel with you, then, where will you take me?"

"We will start, I think, with the home where I grew up. Then perhaps you can meet my tutor. After that, well . . . I'm going too fast and will spoil the ending if I tell you all about what we are to do, where we are to go, and who we are to meet." He smiled broadly. "Are you ready, Tom?"

"Mr. Lewis, I mean, Jack . . . I'm dying." I don't know why I said this. There was something about this man that moved me to open up to him.

"Yes. Sometimes we must lose our life in order to find it. Everyone is dying, you know—or has died. Most people, if you think about it."

"But in my case death appears to be happening sooner rather than later."

"That changes nothing, Tom. You may be pleased to know, however, that when you are with me, you will feel healthy, though I do not guarantee that you will be free from weariness or other minor discomforts that come with a mortal body; I merely mean to say that for a time your illness will not interfere with your ability to travel with me."

I paused a moment, checking myself—diagnosing myself, really. Maybe it was the nap or the medication, but this man, whoever he was, did seem to be speaking the truth about my health. I felt fine. More than fine—I felt wonderful. It was as though the disease that had been killing me was, at least for now, gone. If I had believed in miracles, I might have considered my current state of health to fall into such a category. But no, of course I felt fine. After all, this must be a dream or a hallucination, and this stranger the result of some undigested bit of beef. Whatever the case, I decided, primarily out of curiosity, to follow its course.

"You don't believe in me?" asked the man.

"I believe that the brain is capable of playing tricks," I said, "especially when one is ill."

"What evidence would you have of my reality, then?"

It was a good question, but I didn't have an answer. My skepticism left little room for belief in this man, but I couldn't think of what would make the situation any more real to me.

"I'm not sure what evidence would convince me, Jack," I said. "Maybe if you showed me something—out of the ordinary?" It was more question than statement. "Anyway, how do we get to where you want to go? If a nurse sees me leave this room, I'll be brought back immediately." *And,* I thought, *I probably won't get dessert with my next meal.*

"That's the fun part," said Jack, smiling and turning his head to the right, toward the window, snow still falling outside.

Suddenly a large, ornately carved wardrobe appeared in the room, blocking my view of the window. I hardly need remark at this point that I was certain I had either lost my mind or was experiencing a vivid, though interesting, hallucination. Yet, there it was—a wardrobe in my hospital room. I recalled the famous book by Lewis called *The Lion, the Witch, and the Wardrobe.* If memory served correctly, a little boy—or was it a little girl?—entered a fantasy world by stepping through a wardrobe. The child then met a mythical creature. Was it a faun or a dwarf? I couldn't remember.

As if he knew my thoughts, Jack said, "Of course in my story the little girl—Lucy—entered a fantasy world. We, however, will now enter the reality of my world—the reality of my past and its relevance to your present and future."

The man stood up and walked over to me. He stretched out his hand, beckoning me.

"The time has come," the stranger said, "to talk of many things."

It really was like something out of a fantasy story. I got out of bed and took a hesitant step toward Jack, as I quickly stepped into my cheap hospital slippers. They were pink—the only color they had left, or so the nurse had told me.

"It's all right," he said kindly, like a doctor speaking to child who was about to get an injection, I thought. "I wouldn't have been sent if it wouldn't be all right."

My thoughts were too jumbled to ask who or what "sent" him. The man—Jack—took my hand, walked to the wardrobe and opened the door. Inside I saw what looked like fur coats of many colors and sizes. Jack stepped in first, making a gap between the hanging coats, then I followed, making sure to leave the wardrobe door open. Everyone knows what a foolish thing it would be to get locked in a wardrobe.

As I pondered the utterly ridiculous situation I found myself in—

walking through a wardrobe with a lunatic, my body clothed in nothing but a hospital gown, my feet shod only with flimsy pink slippers—I suddenly realized that we were no longer in my room. We were out in the open, in broad daylight (where had the blizzard gone?), standing before a large Victorian-looking home.

"Welcome to Little Lea." Jack smiled, gesturing to the home. "Ireland."

We Visit Jack's Childhood Home

Wherein we visit Jack's childhood home in Ireland, discuss his father, converse about the meaning of longing, and I am accosted by a small dog, aptly named.

I blinked as my eyes adjusted to the bright sunlight. A cool breeze seemed to assure me that I wasn't dreaming. It also reminded me that I was wearing nothing but a hospital gown. I noticed the open wardrobe behind me and could just make out my darkened hospital room visible through the wardrobe, but had no time to dwell on this strange scene. I heard noises and looked in the direction of a garden. Two boys were eagerly digging a hole.

"Jack, can they see me?"

"No." He hesitated. "At least, I don't think they can see you. Why do you ask, Tom?"

"It's just that I'm not exactly dressed for the outdoors."

"Quite right." He paused and thought for a moment, raising his right hand to his chin.

"Take a coat."

"What?"

"A coat—from the wardrobe." He gestured with his hand.

I turned and looked at the fur coats hanging in the wardrobe. There were many large ones, almost like kingly robes. Thinking I'd be better off with a fur coat over my gown, I reached for a large brown coat and slowly put it on. Its weight felt comfortable on me, but I don't think my appearance was much improved by it. Jack glanced at me, but said nothing about it.

In an effort to move the conversation away from the direction of my clothing, I asked, "What are those boys doing?" I could, in fact, see well enough what they were doing. Covered in dirt, they were digging a hole and laughing.

"They're digging, of course," said Jack, smiling.

"Why?"

"We're looking for a pot of gold."

He carefully stressed the word *we're*, indicating, I surmised, that he was one of the boys. This will be an interesting dream, I thought. After all, it's not every day that one gets to ask C. S. Lewis questions.

The breeze brought a slight chill to my face, though I was warmer now with the coat on. In a mirror in the wardrobe door I saw how ridiculous I looked, but had no time to contemplate my appearance further. The noises coming from the direction of the garden had again captured my attention.

"Who are they?" I asked.

"That larger boy on the right is my brother, Warren—" began Jack.

"And the other boy is supposed to be you?" I interrupted, my tone skeptical.

"Yes, that's right."

"So you're saying we've traveled back in time? That's impossible, you know." I spoke cautiously, being careful not to offend Jack. I still believed myself to be delirious, dreaming, or both, but there was no point in aggravating an illusory person.

"Not exactly, but it appears that way. It is more, I think, what you might call a reenactment rather than time travel."

"I see," I said, though I really didn't. "And why do those boys—you and your brother—think there is a pot of gold buried in this garden?"

"Earlier that day we had gone for a walk with our nursemaid, and we saw a rainbow and imagined that it ended in our front yard. I convinced Warnie that it would be a good idea to pretend we were digging for a pot of gold. This is Ireland, after all—with leprechauns, from the Old Irish meaning 'small body,' a troublesome sprite."

"I know what a leprechaun is, Jack."

"Of course."

The boys were digging hurriedly and, not surprising, the hole was getting bigger and bigger.

Suddenly a small dog bounded in our direction, barking rapidly.

"I thought you said we couldn't be seen," I said to Jack. The dog was now sniffing at my feet and growling.

"Well, I guess Nero can sense us," Jack replied. "And maybe others."

"Others? Nero?"

"The dog. We named him Nero. I forget why."

"I can think of some reasons." I smirked, as the dog continued to sniff and growl at my feet, occasionally nipping at me.

"Put your hand out—gently, like this," said Jack, extending his hand carefully before the dog, who sniffed then licked it, all the while wagging its tail.

"You can touch him?" I asked, surprised. For some reason I didn't expect to be able to interact with beings in this "reenactment," as Jack called it.

"Apparently," Jack replied. "Nero, run along now," said Jack, as he knelt and affectionately patted the dog's head. It appeared to smile, its tongue hanging out, and the animal tilted its head to one side. The small but formidable beast—a Sheltie mix—looked up at Jack, wagged its tail, and ran off toward the boys.

Glad to be free of the canine menace, I turned my attention to the diggers—young Jack and Warren, according to Jack. It looked as though they had finished with their digging, producing a rather large hole in their front garden. A female voice from inside the home called to them, and they ran into the house through what I suspected was the main entrance.

"Let's jump ahead a bit," said Jack. "Nothing of much interest will happen for several hours." I noticed some clouds in the sky moving rapidly, the sun changing position, Nero running in the yard—back and forth—at a rapid rate before he entered the house. Then everything slowed once again to a normal pace. It now appeared to be late in the afternoon, as it was getting dark.

I then noticed a figure approaching the front gate. As he got closer I got a better look at the man. He looked to be about Jack's height, perhaps a little taller, but unlike Jack in his rumpled clothing, the man wore a clean, well-pressed suit, complete with tie and vest, and also sported a black bowler hat. His bushy dark mustache—which made it appear as though the man had no upper lip whatsoever—and unsmiling face did not invite friendliness. A man of business, I guessed.

He walked briskly, no doubt eager to get home after a work day. I noticed, however, that he was walking directly toward the large hole. Before I could shout to him to stop, he fell in. After some grunts and other indecipherable noises, he struggled to climb out, finally getting a good hold on one edge and lifting himself out of the hole. His fine suit was now crumpled and covered with fresh dirt, and his hat was nowhere to be seen. He did not look pleased as he marched determinedly to the front door.

"My father," said Jack, smiling slightly but also looking somewhat wistful. "He was not pleased. I tried to explain that we were merely imagining there was a pot of gold in our yard and, quite naturally, that we were looking for it, but he would have none of it. He thought we had deliberately set a trap for him."

"What happened?" I asked.

"Our nurse, Lizzie Endicott, later threatened to spank our 'piggie-bottoms,' though she never did. Ironic, really, considering that we had gotten the idea from dear Lizzie in the first place. She was the one, you see, who regaled us with all kinds of stories, including one about a leprechaun and a pot of gold at the end of the rainbow."

"I see. Your father—"

"Albert."

"Albert was a man of business?"

"Oh my, yes. He was a solicitor—what you would call a lawyer. A fine lawyer, too. He had a great gift for rhetoric—a person of passion. He was a nineteenth-century man, of course, born in 1863, during your Civil War."

"You got along well with him?" I sensed some difficulty in Jack's tone when discussing his father.

He stared at me for a moment. "Well enough, I suppose, though our relationship was strained for many years. It improved later. He was a good man, as far as men can be called good. He loved books and rhetoric. He could talk politics with the best of them. And yet . . ." Jack paused, a quizzical expression on his face. "And yet, he could not pronounce the word *potato.*"

"Excuse me?"

"Potato. He couldn't pronounce it. His particular Irish accent resulted in *potato* being pronounced something like 'pudaita.' Warnie and I used to call him 'Pudaita-bird,' though not to his face. It was my father who had this home built for us—Little Lea." Jack gestured to the large home.

"In 1905, the year I would turn seven, we moved in."

It was indeed a large home. I counted at least five chimneys from our position, though there may have been more. Its vibrant red bricks contrasted nicely with the white trim on the windows, the surrounding greenery—trees, shrubs, flowers—and with the clear but darkening blue sky. I had never been to Ireland and, in fact, did not believe I was there now. But what I saw was, nevertheless, beautiful. It was a quiet, peaceful location. I could not hear any cars or airplanes or other noise I was accustomed to hearing. It felt strange, yet calming.

"This home—Little Lea—means a lot to you?"

"Yes and no," said Jack. "Like most children, Warnie and I became attached to our home. Because of all the rain and parental fears that we'd catch cold outdoors, we spent a lot of time inside—playing, creating, reading. My parents loved books and, as a result, our home was filled with them. We had no television, radio, or that monstrosity you people call the Internet. They were different and, I'd argue, in many ways, better times for children—at least when it came to our education.

"It was in this home that Warnie and I invented Animal-Land. I called it Boxen. We told stories of mostly political intrigue involving clothed, talking animals. We also spent hours drawing and reading. No book was off limits to us, though I dare say there were many we were too young to understand. I was nine or so when I first read Milton's *Paradise Lost.* We had a wonderful space to ourselves in the attic—our 'Little End Room,' we called it. There is the window—" Jack pointed to the home, at a window on an upper level.

"Looking back I see that the struggle between my reason and imagination began very early on," continued Jack. "In some ways imagination satisfied—but only in brief glimpses of joy—my desire and longing for something outer and other. In German this feeling of longing is sometimes called *Sehnsucht,* which is similar in some ways to what one might call nostalgia, but it is much more and much deeper. It is really a longing or desire for the transcendent—for God, for heaven, for the country we were really made for . . . our true home. But most people do not realize this."

Jack stopped suddenly, breathing deeply. He began to walk slowly around the home, with me walking beside him, my pink slippers an eyesore on the rich green grass.

"And as a child you felt this—desire?"

"I did. I think many children do, though they grow up and often forget or associate their longings with nostalgia rather than stopping to think and analyze what it could really mean for them—indeed, what it could mean for the human race."

"But I don't understand how this longing makes the case for God or heaven. It seems a bit of a stretch."

"To present a simple version of my argument, I would say that if human beings have longings that nothing in this world can satisfy, the logical conclusion is that we were made for another world—for somewhere else."

"I still don't see how that argues for God. And I don't think it is a logical conclusion. Longings could mean a lot of things," I said.

"Well, you get hungry now and then, I take it?"

"Yes. Everyone does—it's part of our biological nature."

"And when you get hungry you eat because there is food to be eaten?"

"Naturally."

"Well then, if we have spiritual hunger that cannot be satisfied by anything in this world, I think a good case can be made that we were made for another world—a world that will satisfy our true longings and desires. We were made for God—for joy. Augustine and Pascal hinted at this argument. In fewer words than I used, they understood and communicated the nature of this longing."

"I'd like to hear more about what they said."

"Perhaps later. I think they touch powerfully upon our predicament as human beings. We are trying to fill the void of our longings with everything except God. Even the longings of a child point to this grand fact. That is why when my brother Warnie one day showed me a toy garden that he had made, I was struck by this feeling of desire and joy. For me the toy garden, crude as it was, stirred within me this longing for more. It would be many years before I would figure that out."

Jack had given me much to think about, but I wasn't convinced. This longing could be any number of things. I didn't see that it had to be God. Just because someone longs for something better doesn't mean that God exists.

"I can see that you're not convinced," said Jack, probably reading the expression on my face. "No matter. We can discuss this again later. Perhaps once you've seen more of my life you'll understand my argument a bit better. It ties in as well to the reality of heaven and of our immortal nature."

Before I could reply, a woman's voice coming from inside the home distracted me.

"Albert, dear," the voice said, "I don't think it is reasonable to assume the boys deliberately set a trap for you." I heard a dog bark several times.

"Please put that beast outside!" said Albert. I looked to the front entrance as the door opened. Nero ran out, fortunately not in our direction, as a woman stepped briefly outside. The woman, whose hair was up, wore a long sleeved white blouse buttoned to the top, a large dark bow around her neck, and a long dark skirt. I saw her face, plain but kindly, as she watched the dog run off toward the garden, before she turned and went back into the home, closing the door behind her. She looked to be in her midforties, maybe younger.

"My mother—Flora," Jack said. "She was the reasonable one in the home. It couldn't be helped, what with her degrees in logic and mathematics. We had, on the whole, good parents, a wonderful place to live, delicious food to eat, and, despite the large hole in the ground—" Jack said, pointing, "a fantastic garden."

"It sounds like you had a pleasant childhood."

"We did, but like many things in this world, it was not to last. When I was nine years old, my mother became ill. Doctors and nurses came and went, sometimes in the middle of the night. One evening I remember having a toothache and going to see her late in the evening, but I could not get to her."

"What was wrong with her?"

"Cancer."

I swallowed hard, thinking of my own precarious condition. The doctors were optimistic, but I knew these things could change in an instant.

"An operation occurred, in our home," Jack continued, "in February 1908. She seemed better for a time, but by August that year—" He broke off and turned away.

"She did not recover, then?" I asked quietly.

"No. On August 23, my father's birthday, she died, and with her death my world showed its true colors—a feeble house of cards . . . with my mother's death it came crashing down. Oh how I prayed she would recover! When she died I even prayed for a miracle—that somehow, like Lazarus, she would rise from the dead and once again be my loving—and living—mother. Warnie and I, naturally, took the news very hard. My father, however, was emotionally devastated by the loss. I don't think he was prepared to deal with my mother's death. Within a few weeks he sent us to boarding school."

"Jack, I am truly sorry, but why exactly are you telling me all this?"

"Because, Tom, you need to know, that I too know grief and pain. I know what it is like to lose the ones I love."

I frowned slightly. What was Jack getting at? What did he know about me?

Jack continued, "I know how cruel this world can seem at times. It is the evil in this world that drove me to atheism. How could God allow it?"

Now Jack was speaking my language. He was right. If a loving God exists, as Christianity claims, and if this loving God is all-powerful, then why is there so much evil in the world?

"It's a classic argument against the existence of God, you know, and I think it's a good one," I remarked.

"Yes, it is a classic argument, as you put it. As old as humanity, I would wager. And yet, it is, in the end, really a hollow argument against God."

"How so?"

"Come, let's speak of it somewhere else. But first, I think we will skip my horrid boarding school years and jump ahead to a more pleasant and fruitful educational experience."

I followed Jack as he began to walk beside his childhood home. As we turned a corner everything changed. Little Lea was gone. We were now in a train station—an enormous black steam engine, passenger cars in tow, loomed before us.

"Now this is the way to travel," Jack said, grinning. We boarded the train, found a compartment all to ourselves and soon were on our way.

3

Atheism and a
Man I Can Relate To

About our encounter with William Kirkpatrick—Jack's former tutor—with whom we discuss atheism and education, and, despite my attire, I am complimented.

The train slowed, then stopped.

"Jack, where are we?" The ride had been pleasant enough, with Jack talking about his studies at Oxford and his brief stint as a substitute lecturer in philosophy, but he had not told me where we were going.

"Bookham station," said Jack as he looked through our compartment window. I, too, looked and saw an old train station.

"Why did we bother to take the train?" I asked. "I mean, couldn't we have just appeared here without it?"

"Of course, but what fun would that be!" exclaimed Jack. "I'm afraid your culture moves too fast for me, Tom. Even in my day people were always in a hurry to get places. I could never understand this behavior—rushing from place to place, missing the joys of the journey. That's why I always appreciated a nice, slow train ride. Do you know that when buying a railway ticket I would sometimes ask the clerk for the slowest train? At any rate, I always enjoyed travel by railway. Sometimes I would get a compartment all to myself—an excellent time to read or think or say my prayers."

We got up and exited the train. Jack motioned to a couple of bicycles leaning against the station building. "Those will do fine," said Jack as he approached a bicycle.

"Jack, I don't think I can ride in these clothes." Jack glanced in my direction, no doubt amused by my fur coat, with bits of my hospital gown poking through the bottom.

"Quite right. A nice walk will do us good, then. You might want to acquire some better footwear if the opportunity arises," he added, looking down at my pink hospital slippers.

We began our walk through the wild countryside. It had been a long time since I took a walk, enjoying the stillness—the sounds of birds, the occasional ripple of running water. It was quite a change from my dreary hospital room, where looking out my window, it seemed winter would never end. After a short time of silence, Jack spoke.

"I owe a great debt to the man we are about to meet," he said. "Intellectually speaking, he sharpened my skills like no one else. He had a gift for knowing exactly how to teach individual pupils. Education today has, to a large extent, lost that gift."

"How so?"

"Can one really expect to place thirty or more students in a room with one teacher—no matter how capable—and expect education specifically tailored to each student? Does knowledge—the memorization of facts and such—amount to intellectual wisdom? Some students are always left behind, while others are bored from not moving ahead. But my time here—" He paused, stopped walking for a moment and gestured to our surroundings. "My time here was something special indeed. I must, however, warn you that the man we are about to meet is not to be trifled with in conversation."

Some time later we arrived at an old home. An elderly man was working in a garden, kneeling in the dirt and working it with his hands with seeming relish.

"Where are we?" I queried.

"Gastons, he called it—my tutor, that is, William Thompson Kirkpatrick or, 'the Great Knock,' if you prefer. This is his home."

"Your tutor?"

"Yes, the Great Knock—he was an expert at knocking down arguments, you see. He tutored me from 1914 to 1917. He used to be headmaster of a college in Ireland. He's an atheist, by the way, and, I might add, an extremely logical person."

"Good," I replied. "I think I will like him, then."

"We'll see," said Jack, with some amusement in his tone. We walked over to Kirkpatrick.

"Good day, isn't it?" I said, deciding it was time I took the initiative in these conversations.

Kirkpatrick looked at me with keen eyes. He was still kneeling, his hands working the earth. The sun glittered on his balding head; he had more hair on his face—his sideburns, which connected to his mustache, were white and bushy. Jack later told me this look was in fashion at the time—side whiskers they called them.

"Stop!" The elderly man nearly shouted, startling me. "Good?" he said in a hoarse but powerful voice as he stood up. The tall, strong man wore, like Jack, a somewhat shabby looking suit.

"What do you mean by 'good'? What is it about this particular day that you find 'good'? Have you been to Surrey before?" I shook my head.

"Thought not." I thought I heard him mutter "Americans" under his breath, but wasn't quite sure. "How do you know what makes a 'good' day here or anywhere else?"

"I just meant that it's a nice day, you know, to make conversation."

"Ah," he sighed. "Conversation. Unless it has a greater purpose and is based on the laws of logic, I see no need for conversation." He knelt again and began working in his garden, eagerly digging in the earth with his hands, like a child in a sandbox. After a few moments his attention turned to Jack.

Kirkpatrick looked up surprised, as if noticing Jack for the first time. "Jack? Is that you, my boy! What has brought you here? I thought you had moved on to your fellowship at Oxford. Really, Jack, you must give an old man some advanced notice of such a visit."

"My apologies, Kirk." Jack smiled and shook Kirkpatrick's dirt-covered hand.

"Well, it's good to see you, nonetheless, but you're looking more worn than when we last met. Are you sure you are well? My, it has been a long time!" said Kirkpatrick as he stood again, his powerful yet lanky frame causing us to look up at him. "Let's see . . . you were but sixteen when I first saw you, weren't you, lad?"

"Something like that," answered Jack, wiping his soiled hand on his pants.

"Then, despite my rigorous tutoring," Kirkpatrick said, frowning, "I hear you went off and became a Christian."

"Yes, I did. It was, you see, the most logical option left open to me," replied Jack.

Kirkpatrick said nothing to this, but still wore his frown.

"And who is this?" He gestured to me. "He seems to think it is a 'good' day, at any rate."

"Clerk. Thomas Clerk. Meet Mr. William Kirkpatrick."

"And why, Mr. Clerk," he said, offering no handshake, "are you wearing a fur coat on a warm spring day?" I had forgotten about the coat, but now that it had been brought to my attention, I not only felt foolish but also warm.

"It's complicated," I answered, feeling embarrassed as I removed my coat, placing it on the ground. Kirkpatrick stared briefly at my hospital gown, glancing down at my now dirty pink slippers, but said nothing.

"And what, other than presumably a train and your feet, brings you here?"

"I'd like to discuss a few thoughtful things with you," said Jack. "Education, logic, atheism."

"Thoughtful talk is the only kind worth bothering about. I am at your disposal, then, gentlemen." He wiped his hands on his pants, clearing some dirt away in the process, folded his arms and said, "What is it that you would like to know?"

"What was your approach to education?" asked Jack.

"To educate. To teach. To help my pupils discover and use their talents to the best of their abilities. And to get them into the right schools—to pass the exams. That's what the parents paid me for, at any rate. It worked with your brother, Warren, much to your father's surprise, and with you, too, as I recall. Everyone possesses the ability to be a great thinker, but most don't take the time to make it so. You, on the other hand, Jack, relished your time here."

"Indeed. Considering my nightmarish experiences in boarding schools," Jack said as he laughed, "coming here was—refreshing."

Jack's jovial nature struck me as out of character. I guess I had expected a serious scholar, frowning as he graded papers. But Jack's good nature—his kind smile and laugh—told more about him than one could read in a book or see in a photograph.

"Well, I'm glad you found your time here of use," said Kirkpatrick. "Your brother, Warren, wasn't too keen on being here at first."

"Different temperaments, I think you will agree," offered Jack, "require different educational approaches."

"At times, yes. And what did you learn here, Jack?" queried Kirkpatrick.

"French, Greek, Latin, some Italian and German, too, I think."

"Ah yes, languages. Important for grasping the classics properly. I believe you studied classics here as well?"

"Of course, as you well know. Homer and such. Cicero—what a bore! Dante, Heroditus, Lucretius, Sophocles, Tacitus, Virgil and the rest."

And the rest? Jack had just rattled off a list that would put most public school students, no matter how smart, to shame. I'd heard of some of the names he mentioned, Cicero and Dante of course, and Sophocles, but I doubt I could express much about their ideas. I had a feeling that Jack, on the other hand, could quote them at will, if need be.

"You preferred enlightenment rather than ignorance," said Kirkpatrick. "An admirable trait in any young man. And what of Schopenhauer?"

That name I had heard in college. One of my professors—Dr. Danzig—liked to praise Schopenhauer, something about a principle of sufficient reason, will as reality, life as suffering, and letting go of desire; it smacked of Buddhism to me. I never did understand it.

"From Arthur Schopenhauer," said Jack, "one of your favorites, Kirk, if memory serves, I learned, incorrectly, that the universe is the product of chance and that religions are worthless attempts at understanding purely natural forces."

"Incorrectly? How so?" challenged Kirkpatrick.

"The universe is not the product of randomness, and neither is religion worthless."

"First point. The universe. Expand, please." Kirkpatrick spoke in short, pointed phrases, like an old-fashioned Western Union telegram, I thought.

"If the universe is a product of random chance, then so are human beings. Agreed?" Jack said.

"Yes."

"If human beings are the products of random chance, then so are their intellects—their minds. Agreed?"

"Naturally," replied Kirkpatrick.

"Then why should we trust our reason?"

Kirkpatrick paused. He did not appear shaken, though I admit that Jack had thrown me into some mild confusion. Being an atheist and, in turn, denying anything supernatural, I agreed that the universe was simply the product of chance and time. Certainly it was improbable that randomness would result in a habitable planet and creatures such as human beings, but here we were so it must have happened, given enough time and the proper ingredients, so to speak. But Jack's comment about trusting our reasoning abilities, assuming they were in fact the products of chance, was a bit jarring. Nevertheless, I was sure there had to be a good atheistic response to such an accusation.

"We trust our reason not because of its origin," countered Kirkpatrick, "but because we know that it works."

"Stop!" Jack held up a hand, in playful imitation of his former tutor. "Let us go no further until we settle the matter of why we should trust human reasoning if it is the product of randomness. On the basis of your atheism—your naturalistic take on reality—everything is a product of chance, including your mind. Why trust logic? Its origins are chance and time."

"You are trying to befuddle me," said Kirkpatrick.

"I already have." Jack smiled. "And to 'befuddle' means one is unable to think clearly, which is exactly my point. On the basis of chance, our minds have no foundation for clear thinking. We have no reason to trust reason. I mean to say that, even though we know reason exists, as demonstrated by our discussion, atheism has no real explanation for its origins, but theism does."

"I hear you," said Kirkpatrick.

"That's his way," said Jack, turning to me, "of acknowledging a good point, without fully giving in to one's conclusions."

"Second point," said Kirkpatrick. "Why are religions not worthless? Is it not true that they are merely primitive attempts by the frightened to understand forces of nature?"

"*The Golden Bough*," said Jack.

"What?" I asked.

"*The Golden Bough*," Jack repeated. "A dozen volumes by James George Frazer, published between 1890 and 1915, if memory serves." Kirkpatrick nodded.

"Frazer's volumes," added Jack, "on comparative religion and mythology, argued, in part, that no one religion was true. Every culture has its own legends, myths and so forth, but Frazer argued that at its core every such belief system has similar myths and legends not unlike what is found in Christianity—a dying god who rises from the dead."

"Quite right," said Kirkpatrick.

"In this way," Jack continued, "Frazer implied that Christianity was really no different than other pagan religions. Magic was the foundation of all religions, from which they all evolve."

"So Frazer shook up the religious establishment," I commented, "by implying that Christianity is not unique—that it, in fact, has much in common with pagan religions?"

"That was one of his angles, yes," said Jack.

"Therefore," said Kirkpatrick, "religions are of no real value."

"That depends," replied Jack. "Later research demonstrated that

Frazer stacked his ideological deck, one might say, in that he read much of his theories into what he studied rather than the opposite—studying, then formulating his theory."

"Really?" objected Kirkpatrick.

"One moment, Kirk," Jack continued. "This 'stacking of the deck' does not concern me much. Let me grant, for the sake of my argument, that Frazer was correct on the point that all religions—or at least a great many—share striking similarities such as a dying god who rises."

"And indeed they do," said Kirkpatrick.

"But does this fact cripple Christianity?" replied Jack. "Hardly! In my estimation it makes sense for God to prepare the way, so to speak, via myths and legends, for the 'true myth' of Christianity—a religion wherein God in the person of Christ dies and rises again. Only this time it is true—it really happened in history and, I would add, in its true expression it is much different—much richer—than the pagan myths, which tend to be cyclical. Christ does not die again and again as a sort of fertility ritual or for the good of our crops. Rather, he died and rose once, for the eternal good of our souls."

"I hear you," said Kirkpatrick softly. "But don't you agree that much of religion is based on fear and misunderstanding of nature? Primitives who know little or nothing of science?"

"My dear Knock, of course many followers of religions—primitive and otherwise—follow or believe out of fear and misunderstanding. This, however, does not mean that there is no truth to the reality of God to grasp. And as to your remark about 'primitives' versus presumably more 'scientific' individuals, I think you would agree that even if science could answer every question there is about the universe—its origins, its 'evolution' and so forth—such scientific answers would move us no nearer to philosophical truth than if we remained scientifically ignorant. Omniscient science still could not answer why there is something—the universe—rather than nothing. Or where everything came from. Or why we exist. Let us not confuse or mangle what science can do and what it cannot do. The great philosophical questions remain, regardless of what science may or may not discover."

Jack had an interesting point. I guess I had never really considered the implications of what he was saying. Supposing science could explain away everything—the existence of the universe, the evolution of intelligent life, for instance—would we still be left with "great philosophical questions," as Jack had called them? But even if that were the case, that would not mean that God must exist, would it? I wanted to give this more thought, but my ponderings were interrupted by Kirkpatrick.

"You mentioned Lucretius earlier, Jack," said Kirkpatrick.

"So I did."

"And what of his argument against the reality of God?"

"'Had God designed the world,' Lucretius said," replied Jack—quoting Lucretius presumably from memory—"'Had God designed the world, it would not be a world so frail and faulty as we see.' What of it?"

"Your response?" queried Kirkpatrick.

"The world is fallen. Things are broken," Jack began. "It is a logical error on the part of Lucretius to assume that the way things *are* corresponds to the way things *have always been* or the way God intended. 'For we know that the whole creation groaneth and travaileth in pain,' to quote Saint Paul's words in Romans. Despite the current fallenness of creation, I believe again with Saint Paul that there is enough evidence of design in the universe to make a case for the existence of God, though I think there are better arguments. 'The invisible things of God from the creation of the world are clearly seen, being understood by the things that are made.' Where Lucretius sees a 'frail and faulty' world, I see a world that corresponds to biblical truth—a groaning world, containing hints of its former glory, but a world that is in need of radical redemption, as are each and every one of us."

I could see Jack's point to a certain extent. But still, I could see the points of the atheists. If indeed creation is broken, granting that a god exists, why was it broken? Could not an all-powerful being create a world without evil or the potential to fall into evil? Before I could voice my questions, Kirkpatrick responded to Jack's argument.

"It appears we are at an impasse, then," said Kirkpatrick. "I disagree with your conclusions, Jack."

"Shall we move on to discuss logic, then?" asked Jack.

"But of course we've already been using logic in our discussion, Jack" Kirkpatrick smirked.

"Right. But what is logic?"

"Logic is the fabric of life—sentient life, at least," said Kirkpatrick, clearly eager to continue this line of discussion. "It is through logic that we not only communicate meaningfully via language, but that we also uncover reality, so to speak."

"So, in your opinion . . ." I began.

"Excuse!" said Kirkpatrick loudly as he held up his right hand, apparently motioning me to stop speaking, and meaning, I guessed, "Excuse me."

"I have no opinions, Mr. Clerk, on any subject. I state facts, I observe reality and interpret it logically."

"So, based on your opin—er, your interpretation of reality," I continued cautiously, "logic is the 'fabric of life' because we use it to communicate meaningfully, to reason, to uncover reality?"

"Correct."

"But does that really answer Jack's question, 'What is logic?'"

"Ah, I suppose it doesn't directly. At least not yet. You have some potential, my boy," said Kirkpatrick, adding, "despite your choice of wardrobe. What do you think, Jack?"

"The laws of logic are readily detectable. Logic helps us think rightly about reality by following some fairly straightforward principles developed, though not invented, by Aristotle."

"Stop!" cried Kirkpatrick. "How are these laws readily detectable and what are they?"

"By saying they are readily detectable I mean they are inherent in any meaningful conversation or process of rationalization," said Jack, slipping into a professorial mode. "They are, as Aristotle articulated, such observations that something is what it is—A is A. Another cornerstone of logic is that something cannot be true and not true at the same time and in the same sense—A is not non-A. Then there is the 'either A or non-A' aspect of logic. For example, either God exists or he does not exist. Finally, I would add the aspect of truth. The statement 'God exists' is either true or false, as is the statement, 'God does not exist.'"

"I hear you," said Kirkpatrick, "but by what means is logic readily detectable?"

"One way is via meaningful conversation," replied Jack calmly. "To communicate and to be understood is to use logic successfully, not in a formal philosophical sense, of course. If I were to say, 'Kirk, hand me the bluspels next to the flalansfere,' we would not be communicating logically unless you understood my language. To communicate meaningfully presupposes logic. It also presupposes that there are entities capable of grasping meaning and communicating it. But if we return to my point about reality being a product of chance, as you claim, then logic, too, is a product of randomness. The origin of reason remains unexplained unless there is an intelligence—an architect—behind it. That is the best explanation."

"Jack, you said that you were once an atheist, right?" I asked, ignoring his reiteration of what I later learned is often referred to as his argument from reason.

"Yes, as you well know."

"What drew you to atheism?" I asked. Jack's journey to faith puzzled me. I could see why Jack, an intelligent man by any reasonable standards, might abandon his faith, but why turn back to it? Kirkpatrick had taught him well, yet while the old man remained an atheist, his pupil had returned to belief in God. As far as I could tell, they had both grappled with arguments for and against God, yet their lives ended up quite different. What was it that moved some to embrace God and others to reject or even deny his existence? On a more personal note, could I trace my path to atheism objectively and, if so, what would I find? Did I reject God because of emotional reasons and only later search for reasons for the rejection, or was there more to it?

"What drew me to atheism?" Jack asked. "Like many things in life, there is no single explanation. In my case, my atheism was brought about by many factors—intellectual and emotional. The death of my mother certainly was a contributing factor. Intellectual obstacles regarding the reality and existence of evil also contributed. My time here with the Great Knock," Lewis said, nodding in Kirkpatrick's direction, "while not overt tutelage in atheism did expose me to ideas that would tend to support atheism. Schopenhauer and Frazer, for instance, did nothing to support firm belief in Christianity. There was also a certain amount of moral disagreement and pride on my part. I did not want some interferer telling me what to do and not do or how to live my life."

"To be fair, I did not force atheism upon you," said Kirkpatrick. "I don't think I mentioned it at all."

"Quite right. Your job was to prepare me for getting into Oxford—a job you completed admirably and one for which I am greatly in your debt. The answer to your question, Tom, is a complicated one. What makes anyone an atheist? Kirk here used to be Presbyterian—and why he still wears his nicer clothing on Sundays is beyond me!" I thought I saw Kirkpatrick blush, but only for a moment. Jack continued, "I, too, grew up in a home of Christian background. There are many reasons for atheism, but there are many reasons for theism as well."

"Then how does one decide?" I asked, sincerely.

"That is the question," said Jack. "We strive, we seek, we find—we do not yield, if I may be so bold as to paraphrase Tennyson. We examine the evidence, we weigh it, we follow it wherever it leads. In my estimation, the best evidence leads to God. Christianity is the best explanation of reality. That is not to say that it is flawless, but compared to other systems, it is indeed a much better solution."

With that, our conversation with Kirkpatrick came to a close. Jack and Kirkpatrick exchanged handshakes and smiles—not animosity regarding their differences as I expected. They had learned, it seemed, to have their disagreements, which were indeed significant, but also to remain friends and to remain cordial. We left, walking again. I turned back and saw Kirkpatrick once again kneeling and working in his garden.

I walked a short while in silence with Jack. Our discussion with Kirkpatrick had given me much to consider. Then a low rumbling noise stirred me from my thoughts.

"What's that?" I asked Jack, looking around for the source of the noise.

"One moment," said Jack, holding up a hand as he listened intently. The rumbling sound grew louder.

"It's the bombing in France. Sometimes when it is very quiet you can hear it even from Great Bookham." But the sound had grown louder—

too loud in fact to be far away. It seemed almost on top of us.

Then it suddenly became darker, as though it were the middle of the night. No longer did I hear rumblings, but many loud noises—explosions, the sounds of whistling in the air followed by more bombardments.

Jack's face went white. "I know these sounds," he said, loud enough that I could hear him despite the explosions around us. "We are in France. The Great War—the war to end all wars—is underway, Tom, and has been for a few years now. I'm sorry to say that you are about to witness firsthand the evils of warfare. We must be careful."

❧ 4 ❧

Evil in the Trenches

In which we discuss peace, war and the problem of evil, while journeying through the trenches of World War I in France; I also find better footwear.

"France?" I asked.

"Yes, the front lines if I'm not mistaken. World War I."

I looked around. We were in a long trench that stretched in two directions as far as my eyes could see, which was not too far because of smoke and dust. I coughed.

"Unbearable, isn't it? And yet, many endured. Yes, hundreds of thousands died, including my friend Paddy Moore." He paused, then spoke more softly. "But many survived. Speaking of which, you're really not dressed for survival in the trenches."

Jack was right. I had almost forgotten that I had left my coat at Kirkpatrick's house, where the weather was quite warm. I was back in my pitiful hospital gown, which offered little protection against the cold night air, and my slippers would have a hard time in this rough terrain. Jack was rummaging through a sack in the corner.

"Here, put this on. Better take the helmet and boots too." Jack handed me a somewhat worn World War I uniform, the helmet and boots. I put the uniform on over my hospital gown and discarded my pink slippers, not sorry to see them go.

"So this is warfare?" I asked, my voice shaky despite my best efforts to remain calm, as I placed the helmet on my head.

"Not just any kind of warfare, though all have their horrors," continued Jack, "but trench warfare. Are you familiar with it?"

"Not really," I said, "at least not more than what little I studied of it in my school days."

"It's fairly straightforward. Two opposing enemies face off in trenches. The area between the opposing trenches, called 'no man's land,' could be as short as just a few dozen yards or perhaps as long as a few hundred or more. That, however, is an oversimplification of what really happens in trench warfare."

"How so?"

"Well, the living conditions, for instance, were deplorable. Mud, filth, blood, diseases brought on by parasites—all this and more encompassed our lives. Even what you might consider a minor injury in your day could result in death in the trenches because of infection and poor medical assistance. The injured sustained most of the wounds as a result of shelling—fragments of metal blasting into our bodies. I was hit and, believe me, Tom, it hurt. Eventually no man's land became littered with bodies from both sides—mangled bodies, due to the shelling, often prevented us from identifying the remains. I once compared the sight of dying men to that of insects—beetles—half-crushed, yet living, though not for long. Sometimes the opposing sides would agree on a temporary truce in order to retrieve the wounded. Your General Sherman got it right when he likened war to hell."

"It sounds horrible. How long did you fight in the war?"

"Five months in the trenches—five months longer than I would have liked! I arrived on the front lines on my nineteenth birthday—November 29, 1917." He looked serious, then added, "Follow me."

We walked carefully through the trench. Every now and then we stepped over a sleeping soldier or two. At least I thought they were sleeping. The filth and stench followed us everywhere. We stopped about ten feet from a lone soldier. Now that there was a lull in the shelling, this young man was quietly reading a book.

"Who is that?" I queried, but I already suspected I knew the answer. The man's features, though certainly much younger—leaner, more muscular—were easily recognizable.

"That's me. I used to be in better shape." Jack chuckled. "And I had more hair." He lifted his hands to either side of his head and tugged on his hair a bit, smoothing it down afterwards.

"You're reading a book in the trenches!"

"Of course. There are never convenient moments to study, you know. There's always something going on—some distraction or other. I learned early in life that I could not wait for convenient times or opportunities to pursue my interests. Instead, I made even inconvenient times serve my purposes. Here I was in the middle of a war—what Homer wrote about was dancing, nay, trembling before my very eyes. It was terrifying and exhilarating, horrible and fascinating, the end of the world and the beginning of a new one—the war to end all wars . . . or so we thought. But even in war life goes on. Men must eat, sleep and at times read."

The young man, who did not appear to notice us, indeed was intent on his reading. Despite the filthy uniform, he looked like a boy. At nineteen he may have legally been an adult, but no, there was the face of a boy fighting in a war, fighting in filth, but reading calmly.

"You weren't a Christian at this time?"

"No."

"I've been told that there are no atheists in foxholes—what about trenches?" I asked.

"I never prayed. It would have been beneath my dignity to do so."

"Why did you fight? Were you drafted?"

"No, I fought voluntarily. In fact, since I was technically an Irish citizen I did not have to fight. I believed it was my duty. Not because of any faith element, but simply out of commitment to my adopted home of England. It is a mistake to think that merely because one is an atheist, one has no morals, no loyalty, no courage. Unfortunately, many Christians make this mistake."

"I agree. But how did you cope?"

"Oh, how does anyone ever 'cope' with war? It wasn't really a matter of coping, but of getting through each day somehow or another—enduring, not coping. We had our books, you know, and each other. The worst was never knowing who might be next—who might be next to you, but then gone in an instant or damaged beyond our ability to repair. It was here in the trenches, though, that I began work on my first book. Did you know I wanted to become a great poet?"

I shook my head.

"I did. It is here that I started writing *Spirits in Bondage*. It would be my first book, published in 1919, after the war."

"War . . . did it help justify your atheism?"

"Yes, of course it did. Here I was in a filthy trench, bodies everywhere, some dead, some alive. Rats, lice, disease, constant shelling. If there was a God, it certainly didn't seem like it to me. I mean to say, if a just and good God existed, then why was he allowing this horror?" Jack gestured around us. "In my mind, at the time, I certainly argued that evil and suffering of this magnitude definitely weighed heavily against the existence of God, at least of the Christian sort. Of course, if I had stopped to consider my argument in more detail I think I would have realized it is human beings who cause and continue such wars. Moral agents make their choices and sometimes the choices are evil."

Intrigued, I decided to pursue this topic further. "What changed your mind, then?"

"About God and evil? What is formally known as the problem of evil really needs to be broken down into components. First, I think we should try to articulate just what the 'problem' is. Second, I think we need to realize that the problem of evil is best approached in stages. It is one thing to discuss this important issue from a distance and in philosophical terms—what one might call the intellectual problem of evil—but it is quite another to experience suffering in a powerfully emotional sense. I think it best at this stage for us to emphasize the intellectual aspects. Before we do that, though, what do you see, Tom, as the problem of evil?"

I thought for a moment. After our discussion with Kirkpatrick, I wanted to be sure to articulate my thoughts carefully. After all, Lewis had learned rhetoric in part from a master logician.

"Well," I began, "it seems you've already mentioned the basic problem. It appears that reconciling the existence of evil and suffering with the existence of a good God is a great difficulty. If God really is all-loving and all-powerful—omnipotent—as Christianity says he is, then why does he allow horrors such as war, disease, famine and natural disasters to continue? Wouldn't it be a better world without these things? I mean," I said, almost angry now, my thoughts dwelling again on my own past, "if God is as powerful and loving as you say, why can't he make a world where he can stop these evils or one where they would never occur?"

"Let us consider the options," said Jack coolly. "And remember, as emotional as we may want to become at this stage, I want to address the intellectual problem of evil. I do not wish to minimize the importance of feelings in dealing with evil, but as I said, it is a problem best addressed in stages. Regarding my solution, I don't, of course, purport to be the first to consider these questions and the options. These ideas go back to the Old Testament book of Job, Epicurus, Boethius and so forth, only to be refined by the likes of Hume, Russell and others. I say 'refined,' though sometimes they are merely used for shock value by skeptics these days. Epicurus provided a succinct overview of the options."

"And what would that be?" I asked, eager to get on with the discussion.

"Let us suppose God exists, argued Epicurus. But, as we have already seemingly agreed, evil also exists. Let us say that God exists and he desires to overcome evil. What if God is unable to do so? Or, a more disturbing thought, what if God is able to remove evil, but is unwilling? Another option is that he is neither willing nor able. Christians would say that God is willing and able to take away evil. But still, evil exists."

"Right," I remarked. "The better option seems to be that God doesn't exist."

"Wait, Tom, I think you are getting ahead of yourself." A few shells landed in the distance. Jack waited for a break in the noise before continuing.

"Let me share a portion of Epicurus here: If he, that is God, is willing and unable to do away with evil, then he is feeble, which is not in accordance with the character of God. If he is able and unwilling, he is envious, which is equally at variance with God. If he is neither willing nor able he is both envious and feeble and therefore not God. If he is both willing and able, which alone is suitable to God, from what source then are evils? Or why does he not remove them?"

"God seems painted in a corner, assuming he exists," I said.

"Given this line of reasoning, I think it does indeed put God in a difficult predicament. A feeble God—one who cannot control his creation and in fact has allowed evil to exist in it—is not worthy of worship, at least not in a Christian sense. If God is able to do away with evil, but is unwilling to, then perhaps we have a distant and uninterested God, such as one may find in deism. This sort of God merely wound up the universe like a watch and left it to run, while he went on holiday. Or maybe we have an evil God? Or perhaps two gods fighting it out in a cosmic war such as in dualism? But dualism has its own problems. Namely, if we call one of the gods 'good' and another 'evil,' where does this other thing— this standard of morality—come from? It would seem there is a third thing—God—beyond the two dueling gods that is greater than either of them. A First Unmoved Mover, as Aquinas, elaborating on Aristotle, would call this being. Is evil an illusion, then?"

"Of course not." I knew all too well the realities of evil and suffering.

"Agreed. Then we have eliminated pantheists—or most of them, at any rate. Evil is not an illusion—to call it such is nonsense of a most damnable sort. That is to say, those who adhere to the position that evil is an illusion, such as pantheists, are buying into a belief system that, in the end, will most literally result in God's justifiable damnation of them."

"Interesting," I replied. "Those are strong words. The question of damnation—of hell—is something I'd like to discuss with you. But getting back to Christianity, it claims that evil is compatible, somehow, with an all-powerful and all-loving God, right?"

"Yes."

"Doesn't atheism make more sense, given the comments you just made?" I suggested. "Isn't it more plausible that the existence of great evil and suffering is evidence against God?"

"Within the framework Epicurus provides," Jack replied, "it does seem that atheism makes more sense. The question is, does the framework allow Christianity to speak for itself? I think before we continue this line of reasoning, which is indeed important, we need to step back a bit and ask another question. How do you know something is evil?"

"Evil is, well—look around you, Jack! Men being blown to bits is evil. You're just trying to distract me by diverting the issue."

"No, no, Tom, I'm doing nothing of the sort. I promise to return to the issues raised, but I think it important to discuss what evil is and how you know something is evil."

"Well, that's two questions now!"

"Yes, but both are important."

"People know what evil is, I think," I said. "Death, destruction, disease—these are evil. People suffering, children dying, innocent people being killed by criminals, earthquakes leveling remote villages in China. All these things are evil."

"Your examples remind me to make some distinctions," said Jack. "Would you agree that some evil is the result of inter-human affairs? In other words, evils such as this war are the result of human beings fighting with one another. In which case, I don't see how we can rightly blame God for a war that is the result of human actions."

"I would agree that some evil is the fault of human beings," I said.

"I would call that moral evil," Jack said. "But what about some of the other things you mentioned—disease, natural disasters? I would call those natural evils. I think the distinction is important. Responding to the problem of evil involves more than responding to just one aspect of the problem. The solution to natural evil is different, in some ways, than the solution to moral evil. From a Christian point of view, we live in a fallen world. Natural evil, unfortunately, is part of this fallenness."

"But the overall point I am trying to make, Jack—moral evil, as you call it—is that our world is filled with suffering and, as I see it, suffering is evil. If God is good and loving then evil would not be in the world. He would be able to make a world without evil."

"Could he?"

"Yes, he could," I affirmed.

"You may be right." Jack's answer surprised me. "But would such a world be the best world he could make?"

"I don't see why not. I mean, a world without evil would certainly be better than what we have, wouldn't it?" I thought I had cornered Jack, but I was wrong.

"And what if you no longer had the freedom to choose? What if you, Tom, became angry and tried to strike a man with a stick, but before you made contact, the stick turned into a lovely bouquet of daisies? What if God manipulated your mind so that you forgot your anger and instantly became filled with glee? Or perhaps you wanted to share some choice words with someone, out of anger, but God changed your words or manipulated sound waves so that you could not speak until you agreed to avoid the use of harsh words, or instead of angry words, a symphony came out of your mouth?"

"That's manipulation, Jack. I see what you're getting at. You're saying that free will allows for the possibility of evil. That seems like a simplistic answer to something as vast as the problem of evil. I don't buy it. Surely an all-powerful God could have come up with a better way to retain human freedom without the need for evil!"

"You would prefer a race of automatons—of robots, if you will? I wouldn't. The power to choose freely, within the confines of God's sovereignty, is part of what makes us unique beings. Take away this freedom and, frankly, life would not be worth living. Furthermore, pain does have purposes, you know. An often quoted passage in my book *The Problem of Pain* makes this clear. To paraphrase, the world is at times deaf to God.

Pain becomes his way of getting our attention—a megaphone, if you will, to rouse those who cannot hear him otherwise."

"I've had more than enough pain in my life, thank you very much," I said.

"And, no doubt, you will have even more. One thing I find interesting about this argument against God is that it assumes evil exists. But how do you know? By what standard do you know that there is good and evil?"

"You're creating a diversion again."

"No, I am trying to find out the truth," said Jack. "If we are to call something, such as aspects of this particular war and its accompanying atrocities, evil, then there must be a standard by which we judge it evil. You can't call a line crooked unless you know what a straight line is. If we carry this reasoning further, we need to ask, 'Who set the standard?' Then, you see, we are on our way to actually arguing for the existence of God on the basis of the reality of evil."

"Sleight of hand—or word, in this case," I said. "It's a trick."

"Is it? Tom, I believe valid arguments can lead one to truth—that which corresponds to what is real. Trickery is unnecessary, not to mention morally wrong. You say evil exists. I agree. You say evil disproves God. I say evil argues for God. You need to take a closer look at the evidence. My line of reasoning to God follows an intricate progression. It is not based merely on my response to the problem of evil—and I do grant that it is a problem, but not an insurmountable one. For you to call anything evil requires a standard of good. This standard, I argue, is indeed required, and is rooted in the existence of a morally good God."

"Jack," I said, then paused, deciding to take another approach in the discussion. "What about war? Do you think it is ever right?"

"If it is, then there may be times when those who stand idly by and do nothing when one nation decides to overpower another are in the wrong—better for the idle ones to fight the bully, don't you think, so long as a proper leader and government make the decision? I think the question of war is important. It relates to the problem of evil, because war is often brought up as an example of evil in the world. But is war always evil? As a Christian I believe that some things are morally good while others are morally evil. If a nation or group of nations is committing acts of great evil, I believe it is our prerogative as human beings to do our best to stop that great evil. In such cases, war, if decreed by the governing authorities, is justified."

"So pacifism is not an option?"

"It is an option, but in my assessment it is not a reasonable one, especially on the basis of human history and what great thinkers have said on the subject. Do you know, I was once invited to speak to a pacifist society in Oxford? I don't think they liked what I had to say!"

"But didn't Jesus teach his followers to 'turn the other cheek'?"

"Indeed, but what was the context? If you study the passage closely—and similar ones—you will find that Jesus was concerned with personal interactions between individuals in daily life, not war on a national scale. In the Gospel of Saint Luke, Jesus at one point told his listeners to sell their cloaks and buy swords if they did not have them."

"So Jesus sanctioned militant action?"

"No, true Christianity is not inherently militant. Its foundation is love of God and love of neighbor. It is unfortunate that some have used the name of Christ and Christianity for wicked purposes. The goal of true Christianity is not to force belief on anyone, but to give reasoned answers and evidence. War, however, is always with us. It is, in my assessment, up to nations to decide when war is deemed just and for its citizens to obey, so long as obedience does not involve atrocities or going against one's beliefs."

We continued making our way through the trench, stray shells landing here and there in the distance.

"Getting back to the problem of evil, if I understand you correctly, Jack, you are saying that the fact that God is all-powerful can be reconciled with the reality of evil?"

"Yes. It must be if we are to retain the God of Christianity."

"And your argument appears to be that if an all-powerful God did away with all evil, he would have to do away with us, or at least remove our free will."

"But there are some things, Tom, that God cannot do that are a benefit to his nature, not a detriment. He cannot lie, for example, or change, meaning that we can consistently trust what he says and know that he will not change his nature."

"Doesn't that make God less than all-powerful? He becomes the God who cannot lift a rock he created."

"Not at all. It means that God has the capacity to do anything that is in adherence with his nature. He cannot make square circles or lie, for instance. The geometric option is nonsensical, while God's inability to lie is not a deficiency, but a positive character attribute. When it comes to evil, however, I'm not saying God could not do away with it, but to do so would require stripping us of free will or eliminating us all together—both options seem to be evil in and of themselves; so God could not perform them, not to his detriment, but to our benefit."

"I don't know." I struggled to formulate my thoughts. "It seems—it seems that an all-powerful God could come up with a better world."

"It does indeed. But what are the options? Leibniz argued that God could only do his best, so this world must be the best possible world. Aquinas would say this is not the best possible world, but the best way to the best possible world."

"Couldn't God have created nothing?"

"I don't believe God could have created other possible worlds. Some Christian thinkers do, however. In the interest of not being viewed as 'dodging' your question, I shall venture to explore your question. The God of Christian theism is complete in and of himself. He is not dependent on anything and can express love via the Holy Trinity—Father, Son, and Holy Spirit. Therefore, I suppose it is possible he could have not created anything. He created, I think, because he freely chose to do so. But would an uncreated world be better than the alternatives? I don't see how. You wouldn't be here. I wouldn't be here. There would be no creatures with free will."

"But there wouldn't be evil," I said.

"True, but there wouldn't be you, either, or anything else."

"And what if God created a world where creatures lacked free will or God changed their minds whenever their choices would result in evil?" I asked.

"That is a world of robots," answered Jack, "not of freely choosing beings. One of the ingredients, if you will, that makes our current world the best way to the best possible world is that our characters can be formed because of the reality of evil and suffering. This world and our sufferings in it can shape our souls for the better. This world can try us, yes, but also can build us up through our sufferings. This is a world that, if we will give it the chance, can prepare us for eternity."

"How, then, do you avoid the accusation that God is the author of evil?"

"I think the nature of the question puts one in the wrong frame of mind."

"What do you mean?"

"In human terms, you put it as though God is in his cosmic laboratory concocting evil with test tubes and bubbling beakers. The question must first be addressed regarding the nature of evil. Is it a thing that exists on its own? In my view it is a privation—something that is missing. Evil needs goodness to exist, to spoil, but good exists on its own. Evil can only live as a parasite upon the good. God, then, is not the author of evil, as you put it, because evil is not a 'thing' in a proper sense."

"Your answer seems simplistic—evasive, even. You're just trying to get around the reality of God being the author of evil."

"But these are not my original ideas, I merely agree with the likes of Saint Augustine, Saint Thomas and others. I think the answer solves the problem—the accusations—of God being the author of evil. When good that should be somewhere is missing, that is evil. If a man is blind, it is the absence of sight that is evil. If there is a hole in my roof, causing rain to trickle upon me, the roof is not evil, but the absence of goodness, a missing tile perhaps, is evil. This solution does not deny the reality of evil, as pantheism does, nor does it deny the existence of God but affirm evil, as in atheism. Rather, by viewing evil as a privation, I acknowledge its reality, yet deny that God is its author. God created everything, but not the privation of everything. Evil, as I said earlier, is a parasite."

I had little time to ponder Jack's answer, as the shelling picked up again, louder and seemingly closer. Soldiers suddenly began to exit the trench, retreating, it seemed, to another trench in the distance.

"Well, let's go. This trench is about to be blown to bits!" said Jack.

We began a mad dash across a bloody field—no man's land, Jack had called it, but it was full of men now, some running, some falling as they were hit by shrapnel. Smoke and dirt filled my eyes. Jack was running ahead of me, but glancing back now and then to make sure I was following. I stumbled over a shoelace I had not tied tightly enough and collapsed in the mud, losing my helmet in the process. Jack came back, kneeling next to me. The shelling became louder. I looked back and through the smoke I saw enemy soldiers advancing, speaking what I presumed was German.

"Get up!" yelled Jack. He grabbed my left arm, pulling me up. Running wildly we could see a trench just up ahead, but it didn't look like we would make it. I heard a long, low whistling overhead. "Jump!" said Jack. I hesitated. As he pushed me into the trench, my world went black.

5

Can Ideas Destroy Humanity?

In which we discuss Jack's journey to Christianity, talk about mythology, debate on whether or not ideas can lead to the destruction of humanity, and I pull a copy of Dante's Paradiso *off a shelf with surprising results.*

Blackness. I blinked. Still blackness. Still. Quiet. I could hear birds chirping and, nearby, running water—a stream, perhaps. I blinked again, and my eyes were blinded by the brightness of the sun. I was flat on my back. The smoke, dirt and trench were gone. I still wore the uniform of a soldier as well as one of my boots.

Where was Jack? I sat up, checking myself for injuries, and looked around. Jack was standing, quite calmly, surrounded by trees, on a path. I looked around and saw that we were on some kind of trail, beside a river.

"What is this place?"

"Addison's Walk," Jack said, smiling. "It is certainly an improvement over the trenches, don't you think?"

"Of course. Who did you say this walk was named after?"

"Addison. Joseph Addison—a fellow of Magdalen College, Oxford, quite some time ago—seventeenth and eighteenth century by your reckoning. He liked to walk here, hence the name. That's the River Cherwell."

Jack pointed as he spoke. I turned and caught a glimpse of the running water I heard earlier.

"And what brings us here?" I asked, getting up off the ground and wiping the dirt from my clothing.

"Oxford, I suppose—more specifically, Magdalen College. That's it, over there. We can visit the new buildings." Jack pointed. "I served with Magdalen, you know, for many years. Like Addison, I also enjoyed this path. Also like Addison, I was a fellow of Magdalen—a position I first held in 1925. I would remain at Oxford until 1954 when I left for Cambridge, but that is another story."

Jack began walking, with me at his side. Wearing only one boot caused me to stumble a bit, so I removed it, walking barefoot, careful not to step on any sharp stones. I could see why Jack liked Addison's Walk. The lush foliage, the nearness of the river and the bright, warm sunshine contrasted strikingly with the gloominess of the trenches of war.

"It was on this path that I had quite a conversation with Hugo Dyson and Tollers."

"Tollers? Actually, I don't know the name Dyson, either," I admitted, slightly embarrassed.

"Well, Tollers and Dyson were friends of mine. You should meet them."

As Jack finished his sentence, I heard the rustling of some branches up ahead, then voices.

"No, you go on first."

"After you, Hugo."

"No, no, no. Together?"

"Oh, fine."

Two men appeared on the path. One had an unlit pipe held firmly in his mouth, held a walking stick at his side and looked somewhat familiar, but I couldn't place him. The other looked strong—burly, actually—and somewhat balding. His features struck me as those of an eagle: sharp eyes, pointed nose and a head resembling that of a bird of prey.

"Tollers! Dyson!" Jack called out, waving at the men. "How good to see the both of you."

"Jack!" said the burly man. "What brings you to Addison's Walk? You're not going to argue that the Renaissance never happened, are you?" The man laughed. "But who is your traveling companion?" He paused. "I say, his uniform is a bit out of date, isn't it? Are you off to a costume party? You forgot the boots, I think."

The World War I uniform did indeed look out of place on this beautiful path in Oxford.

"Tom, meet Hugo Dyson. Hugo, meet my American friend, Mr. Thomas Clerk. We're on a journey, of sorts. Mostly we've been having some conversations and," he said, "seeing the sights."

"You and your American friends, Jack!" said Dyson, laughing. "How those Yankees dote over you! Ah, I have it now—you are the great Lewis and Clerk on a journey of adventure, is that it!"

I groaned inwardly at the joke, but Dyson seemed a cheerful, genial man.

"A pleasure to meet you, Mr. Clerk," said Dyson as we shook hands.

"And this," said Jack, "is my dear friend, Tollers! You may know him better as J. R. R. Tolkien."

I must have looked quite the fool. My jaw hung open slightly as I stared at the unassuming man standing before me. Here was *the* J. R. R. Tolkien, author of the classic fantasy books *The Hobbit* and *The Lord of the Rings.* I had read them years ago when I was in college and though I found them dry in parts, I was utterly awed by the world this man had created. I hadn't read the books in years, nor any other fantasy literature for that matter, but I knew enough about Tolkien to stand in awe of him. Jack nudged me out of my stupor—Tolkien had extended his hand in greeting—and I shook hands with J. R. R. Tolkien.

"Hello, Mr. Clerk." Tolkien smiled. "And Jack, it is good to see you, but you're looking a bit tired. Feeling ill, are you?"

"I'll manage," replied Jack.

After Tolkien's comment, I looked at Jack and noted that he did indeed look tired. Not so much older, but somewhat worn—not at all like the vibrancy he exuded in my hospital room when we first met. Before I could ask him about it, he spoke.

"I think I know why we are here now, Tom," said Jack, looking at me. "The fact that Tollers and Dyson are here make that point very clear. Surely, you both must remember the many hours in conversation we had one evening long ago. At one point we took our stroll on Addison's Walk."

"Yes, you were quite the stubborn conversationalist," said Dyson. "Oh, you went on and on about the 'Christian myth' and how it could not be true and such. *The Golden Bough* could not help you, not with Tollers in on the conversation—that man knows more about myths than anyone I know! You tried so hard to cling to your atheism, didn't you, Jack?"

"That I did, Hugo, that I did."

"What was it that you called the Christian God, Jack?" asked Tolkien. "Something along the lines of a 'transcendent interferer,' wasn't it?"

"Yes, Tollers, something along those lines. But that night we had our conversation, you both talked sense. By the time we were done, I really had no choice but to believe in Christianity, despite my desire to escape its clutches. Theism, at any rate, had a grip on me."

"Did these men help you understand Christianity?" I asked.

"'Christianity'? Not so much Christianity, but Christ," said Jack. "I did not have some kind of immediate or emotional experience. Weeks passed before I would really consider myself a Christian. But did Tollers and Hugo have an influence in the process of my conversion? Certainly."

"I remember you invited us to dine with you," said Dyson. "We ate, we talked, we strolled on Addison's—"

"Do you remember," interrupted Tolkien, "that strong wind that rustled the leaves?" He looked thoughtfully at the trees around us. "It was a . . . Numenorian moment—the power of God touching the still and warm evening just enough to get our attention." Tolkien paused, looking up at the sky as if expecting the same gust to once again come down from the heavens.

"And enough to get Jack's attention, too," said Dyson. "All that talk about myth, metaphor and pagan stories of dying gods. I remember you left at three in the morning," said Dyson, glancing at Tolkien.

"Well, my wife likes me home by three thirty." He smiled in reply. "But as I recall, you and Jack later told me you talked until at least four."

"Yes," said Jack. "It was one of those evenings of talk and friendship that seemed to pass all too quickly, despite the hours of conversation."

I could tell I was in the presence of three friends. Not wanting to feel too left out, but also wanting to steer the conversation in a direction I could contribute to, I asked Jack, "What was your sticking point with pagan myths?"

"I was fascinated by myths, especially those that gave me a sense of what I called Northernness, and truly enjoyed the longings they stirred in me, especially pagan myths about dying gods coming back to life. Something drew me to them. Balder, son of Odin, and his death and so forth. You know, *Tegner's Drapa* by Longfellow: 'I heard a voice that cried, Balder the beautiful is dead, is dead—' But when I encountered this 'myth' in the story of Christianity—Jesus dying, coming back to life and so forth—it bothered me. I could not believe it."

"You see," said Tolkien, looking at me, "Jack knew deep down inside that there was something more to the story of Christ, but like every human being he struggled with the terms of God. Jack preferred to make his own way, on his own path," he said, pointing to the trail with his pipe, "without the 'transcendent interferer' meddling with his morals. Our pride often gets in the way of so many things, not the least of which is our relationship with God. Jack wanted the stories, but not the truth of the great story that never ends—the story we are in. I think what we helped Jack realize was that Christianity was the true myth." He placed the pipe in his mouth again.

Puzzled, but intrigued, I asked, "Jack, when we were talking with Kirkpatrick you also mentioned the 'true myth.' Isn't a 'true myth' a contradiction?"

"That's the thing, isn't it?" said Jack. "It is God's myth—the true myth."

"But how do you know it is the 'true myth'? There are a lot of myths in the world," I objected.

"The difference, of course," said Jack, "is that I came to believe that the story of Christ, unlike the pagan myths, really happened in history—there is ample evidence for that, if you're willing to look. All these other stories, scattered throughout the centuries and running through countless cultures, really were hinting, faintly at times, at God's true story. You see, the pagan myths captured my attention because they merely hinted at the truth of the story of Christ—the great story of God fully realized in a historical person. We all long for fulfillment in the true story of God. Even though we may think we don't, we try so hard to fill our lives with things—substitutions for God—when in reality we are longing for our true country."

"I don't know," I said. "It still seems to me a far-fetched story, Jesus and the resurrection, I mean."

"How so?" said Dyson.

"The whole thing—a baby born of a virgin, the walking on water, giving sight to the blind, dying and coming back to life. It sounds too much like myth to me—real myth, fables, not this 'true myth' you talk about."

Tolkien took the pipe from his mouth and looked at me for a moment. "It sounds as though your real concern, Tom, is not so much with the story but with the way in which the story incorporates the miraculous. Your naturalism, your denial of the supernatural, is clear." He put the pipe back in his mouth and continued looking at me.

Tolkien was right. I did find the story of Christ interesting, but how could anyone in our modern age accept the miracles that run through the pages of the Bible? And yet, part of me acknowledged that if God existed then miracles could be possible. It was the existence of God that I couldn't get past. There seemed too many obstacles in my way.

"Now, look here, Clerk," said Dyson, "I think you're missing the point—"

"One moment," interrupted Jack. "I think that you two have given Tom enough to think about for now. There's no need to press him further at the moment. I'm sure if he's interested in pursuing this line of reasoning about miracles he might be interested in reading my book on the subject."

"You're right, Jack," said Dyson. "I'm sure Tom has his hands full just trying to keep up a conversation with you!"

I said nothing, but I appreciated Jack's intervention. It's not so much that I did not believe I could hold my own in a discussion with these men, but I was outnumbered and Jack knew it. Instead of cornering me, he had the grace to move on, at least for now. We said goodbye to Tolkien and Dyson and made our way to Jack's rooms at Magdalen College, my mind still working through much of what was said on Addison's Walk.

Magdalen College, Oxford, looked somewhat like a castle from our vantage point. I saw a tall tower with several pointed spires at the top, near a bridge. As we approached the school, I followed Jack down a long hallway—a cloister, he called it. Large, arched windows lined the hall. We took the stairs to the second floor.

Jack opened a door and we entered his rooms. Not surprising, books lined the shelves. They did not look new and unused, as you might see in a retail bookstore, but instead looked old and over-used, if one can say such a thing about books. I scanned collections of medieval English literature, dictionaries, books on philosophy, religion, ethics. I surveyed the room further and saw what looked like comfortable sitting chairs near a window overlooking a green, open field. Looking outside, I caught a glimpse of three deer grazing, then noticed the uncomfortable temperature in the room.

"It's cold," I commented, shivering.

"Yes. There's no central heating system."

"I thought you said these were the 'new' buildings."

"They are. But 'new' to Oxford is not what you think. These buildings were constructed in the seventeen hundreds. I'm afraid there is no central heating system. Let me put some coal on and plug in the space heater. I'll just be a moment."

When Jack returned he was wearing a burgundy robe of some kind. Draped over one arm he held what looked like another robe, but this one was black.

"Here, put this on. You are now an Oxford don or, at least, you are wearing the robes that go with the honor," said Jack as he handed me the academic robe, smiling.

"Thank you. I'll just step into this other room to change." I also wanted to remove the mud-stained World War I uniform, its stench and filth unpleasant reminders of the horrors of war. The robe felt heavier than I expected, as I put it on over my hospital gown, which was still in fine shape considering what we had been through thus far. I heard Jack making a comment from the main room.

"You know, in some literature, characters who wear disguises do so in order to signal to the reader that the character is having an inner identity crisis."

"Well, Jack, this isn't a disguise—I'm just trying to keep warm," I replied as I entered the room, now wearing the black robe of a scholar.

"So, you still believe that atheism is your best option?" Jack said, as he sat down.

"I do," I replied, sitting in the chair near his.

"Despite the fact that it lacks a real foundation for moral values?"

"You keep talking as though atheism has no solid footing when it comes to moral principles," I said.

"In one sense I think it does," said Jack plainly. "Moral standards are evident to everyone. What I find interesting is the fact that certain atheists, such as yourself, want very much for there to be a solid footing, as you put it, for moral principles, and yet I don't see a viable way for you to have it both ways. If God exists, fine, then we can speak of moral principles rooted in his nature. If God does not exist, I don't see a logical solution."

"But that's an oversimplification of my position!"

"What is your position?"

"I believe that even without God, humanity is of value. Improving the human race, wiping out disease, feeding the hungry, overcoming the harsh realities of nature—making real progress. These are the things I believe in. Just because I am an atheist does not mean that I don't care about the world. Given enough time and technological savvy, I think we really can make this world what we want it to be. Free of the enslavement of religion, free of strife and so forth."

"I never said you didn't care, Tom. As an atheist, however, you don't have any real foundation for making the kinds of claims you have made. How can anything be 'good' or 'right' or 'bad' or 'evil' if you have no standard for such concepts? And, goodness, some of the remarks you have made are making me feel as though I am in the heart of the N.I.C.E. itself!" said Jack.

"The what?"

"Have you read my book *That Hideous Strength?*"

"No, I haven't read that one," I said, not wanting to admit that I'd actually never heard of it.

"Well, in that book there is an organization called the N.I.C.E.—the National Institute for Co-ordinated Experiments. Their ultimate goal, known only to those in the innermost ring, is to overcome nature—to become immortal through science and technology. In turn, it represents the rule of some men by others in a world that has lost its moral compass. *That Hideous Strength* represents in fiction many of the points I made in *The Abolition of Man*, though in the form of a story. I subtitled it 'A Modern Fairy-Tale for Grown-Ups.' The N.I.C.E epitomizes the desire of some to break beyond the boundaries of traditional morality and shape the world into what they would want it to be."

"Sounds like a nice place," I quipped. "And you think my comments reflect the thinking of this N.I.C.E.?"

"Not in a fully developed sense, but, you see, I'm always thinking about where certain beliefs will lead, if carried to their logical conclusions. Yes, I think your views, in the end, would fit with the goals of the N.I.C.E. My main point, however, is that as an atheist you need to utilize absolute moral standards in order to accomplish what you'd like, but in order for this approach to make sense, I argue that God must exist."

"I disagree. What's wrong with seeing human beings as valuable and with trying to improve the human race?"

"You're missing my point, I think," said Jack. "But let's grant it for a moment. In your scheme of things the universe will ultimately run down and be no more. What's the point of improving the species, as you put it, if in the end there will be nothing left? I don't disagree that human beings are valuable. As for improving the human race—my comments on that portion of your position will depend on what you mean by 'improving' and how such improvement would be carried out. But let us discuss your comment that human beings are valuable."

"Okay."

"What do you mean by 'value' and on what basis do you determine something is 'valuable'?"

Lewis was a master of Socratic dialogue, as well as rhetoric. He was in 'Kirkpatrick mode' again. I'd have to be careful, but, I thought, I can hold my own in a conversation with him. I was actually finding it refreshing to dialogue with a Christian who not only sincerely believed, but also could articulate and defend his beliefs intellectually. There was no sense of blind faith coming from Jack. I still believed him to be wrong, of course, but there was no doubting his intelligence. I proceeded cautiously.

"By 'value,' I suppose I mean that human beings have inherent worth—the human race, and individual human beings—are valuable."

"And where do you get this standard of value? In other words, what is your view that human beings are of value and have inherent worth based on?"

I had a pretty good idea of what Jack was trying to do. He wanted me to admit that in order for value to have meaning, it had to have a basis in some transcendent source—namely, God. I figured it would be best to respond Socratically myself.

"You're trying to reason me into a corner so that I'll admit that in order for something to have value, there must be a standard by which to determine its value. You think this standard is God?"

"I don't know about trying to reason you into a corner. I'm trying to arrive at truth, at what is real. I want to know on what basis you view human beings as having inherent value and worth. You see, my view that humans are of inherent value and worth is based on my theism. If God exists, and if God is good, and if human beings are made in God's image, then human beings are indeed of value and possess inherent worth. Atheism, on the other hand—even the humanistic variety which you seem to support—has no real foundation for claiming that human beings are of value and worth. Such thinking is dangerous, in the end, because it could have serious consequences for the human race—its destruction or 'abolition,' really."

"I don't necessarily see that as being the case. Just because atheists believe human beings are of value and worth, but do not believe in God, does not mean that such thinking will lead to the destruction of the human race. I really don't see that happening."

"Let me, then, summarize my position. I think you are right in that I haven't really made a thorough case for my position. I will attempt to sketch it for you. Let us say that a group of men and women who deny the existence of God decide that the human race is of value, should be improved and so on. Since they have no real foundation for values—for right or wrong, good or evil—they, in essence, have removed themselves from the inherent moral standards established and rooted in God and his nature."

"That's a bit of a stretch, isn't it?"

"Just follow me for a moment. This group, then, set itself up as the arbiters of what is right and what is wrong, how the human race can be improved and so forth. Ultimately, this will lead to the rule or control of some by others. Given enough time, a philosophy based on these kinds of ideas will lead to practices once considered outrageous and beyond the realm of acceptability."

"That's where you lose me, Jack. Why would that be the case?"

"For one, genetic engineering in order to 'improve' the human machine will ultimately be allowed in such a scheme. In order to mold the human race, one needs material to mold. Infants, even in the womb, will no longer be seen as valuable, but as mere biological tissue to do with what we want. If the elderly become a burden to society, then they must be allowed to do away with themselves or, perhaps, we will do away with them on our own, if a valueless system runs its course."

Jack's words reminded me of contemporary debates about the status of the human fetus, euthanasia, abortion, genetic engineering and so forth. But I still did not see that things needed to end in human destruction, as Jack suggested.

"When men and women step away from absolute moral standards," Jack continued, "rooted in God, they step into the void—an empty world where right and wrong do not really exist in a meaningful way. The human race will be destroyed by such thinking not because absolute standards do not exist—natural law proves that they do—but because men and women of this kind have removed themselves from this realm; they, in fact, are no longer even human as God intended them to be. They become new men for a new age founded not on transcendent, unchanging standards, but on standards that are not really standards at all. Their own desires will shape their behavior. Subjectivism, which is what their beliefs boil down to, carried to its logical conclusions, will lead to the destruction of the human race. Hitler and his ordained 'medical' experiments may have been a human anomaly or they may have been ahead of their time, not in a positive sense, but in one that could lead to our ultimate destruction."

"It seems you are assuming a lot. Won't the actions of such people—these molders—also produce benefits to society?"

"I imagine they would, if by benefits you mean technological and medical advances and such. But I think these so-called benefits come at a cost. We lose our humanity when we deny the reality of moral standards rooted in God. If we follow the path of utilitarianism, where things are done supposedly for the good of the many, then what is to stop the subjection, the oppression, of the few? After all, if it is done for an alleged greater good, then why not kidnap beggars and use them in experiments or begin experimentation on criminals? It is not enough, these molders will say, to merely experiment on animals—cruel as that is—but, they continue, it is time to experiment on human beings, do what we will with them for the 'good of humanity,' clone them if we can, improve their stock and so forth."

"But couldn't moral standards, as you put it, be rooted instead in biology—in evolution, for example? Instincts to help us survive."

"I don't see how that is possible," said Jack. "Moral standards inherently address behavior between personal beings, but a mere biological force in a world without God is random and impersonal. Sometimes, deep down inside, we behave in such a way that goes against our instinctive behavior. At these times we choose to do what we know is inherently the right thing to do even if it may not further our progress, so to speak. We make a conscious choice to do the right thing even when doing the wrong thing may be, from a worldly perspective, more advantageous."

"I still don't agree with your conclusions, Jack. I don't see how ideas can result in the destruction of humanity."

"Perhaps the sticking point is my use of the word *destruction*," Jack said. "I do not mean destruction as in an atomic bomb, but destruction that disfigures our very nature by twisting it into something that it is not. Yes,

I do believe that ideas can destroy us in this sense."

Jack stood, removing his robe, and walked over to one of the many bookshelves.

"Would you do the honors?" he asked.

"What?"

"Have you read Dante's *Divine Comedy?*" Jack pronounced it "dan-tee."

"I read *Inferno* in college."

"In that case, you haven't really read *The Divine Comedy.* To have read one in three is not bad, but you'll want to finish it some day. Ah, here they are. Pull *Paradiso* off the shelf please."

"But you're right next to them." I saw three ornate, leather-bound but worn volumes on the shelf: *Inferno, Purgatorio* and *Paradiso.*

"Humor me."

I stood up and walked over near Jack, reached for the book and pulled it off the shelf. As I did, the entire bookshelf slid open to the left, revealing an ascending and descending staircase.

"I've always wanted to see that happen," Jack said with a smile. "Of course, my real college rooms hid no secret passages, so far as I knew. We're going up. After you—"

"What's down there?" I pointed to the descending staircase and to darkness.

"You don't want to know," said Jack. "And please set the book on your chair."

We walked up the staircase and came to a closed door. Jack opened it, and bright sunlight streamed in. I looked through the doorway and saw a home in a peaceful setting.

"Welcome to the Kilns," said Jack.

"The what?"

"My home."

6

Conversion on a Motorbike

Wherein we visit Jack's home, meet his handyman, discuss salvation and conversion, and make a perilous journey to London by motorbike.

We stepped through the doorway and approached the home. I looked back and saw the doorway leading to the stairs vanish in silence.

"Just a moment," said Jack, as he looked to the skies. "Listen."

Later, of course, I felt foolish for not recognizing the sound. Unlike Jack, however, I hadn't lived through two world wars. At first I thought it was a fire engine, but the sound did not seem to get nearer or further. Besides, it was too long and drawn out to be a fire engine siren.

"It's the air raid siren," said Jack. "We'd better get to the shelter."

"You have a shelter?"

"Yes. I had Paxford build it just in case the bombing ever reached us here."

"Paxford?" I asked. Just then I heard footsteps approaching, then a voice—rustic and earthy.

"Ah, no need for the shelter tonight, Mr. Jack," said the voice. "It's just a drill, not a real raid. Though we, ah, are just as likely to have a real raid tonight, I expect. Well, so much for the Kilns. 'Spect there will be nothin' left of it after the German bombs have 'ad their way."

"Paxford!" Jack smiled as the man approached. He was large and had short, thinning hair. Though his eyes seemed cheerful enough, the rest of his face, double chin and all, looked rather gloomy. He appeared to be about the same age as Jack, but smelled of cigarette smoke and roses.

"Good to see ye, Mr. Jack. And who might this be?" Paxford glanced at me. I hardly looked to be a distinguished colleague of Jack's in the robes of an Oxford don, with my hospital gown peeping through in various locations, my feet bare.

"Paxford, this is Thomas Clerk, an American friend." Paxford nodded, slightly rolling his eyes as if to say, "Ah, American—that explains it."

"And Tom, this is Fred Paxford." I nodded in his direction and smiled weakly.

As Jack later explained, Paxford was gardener and handyman at the Kilns, a position he held for more than thirty years. "Our indispensable factotum," Jack called him. Indeed, apparently Paxford not only did the work of a handyman, but also tended a garden, did some grocery shopping, drove Jack to and from Oxford, performed some rudimentary cooking, tended chickens and more.

The siren in the background suddenly stopped. "It's a drill then?" asked Jack.

"Ah, yes, Mr. Jack, it's a drill. Would ye like to come inside?"

"Not now, Paxford, but perhaps later. You wouldn't happen to have some more appropriate clothing that Tom could borrow, would you? We're going to be taking Warnie's Daudel for a ride to London."

I had no idea what a "Daudel" was, but apparently it offered some kind of transportation. At any rate, I would be glad to get out of Jack's robe and into something more suitable, though I wondered what Paxford would consider "appropriate" clothing.

Paxford glanced at me again, no doubt taking in my ridiculous appearance. He led me to a small structure, presumably his dwelling—a bunga-low, I think he called it. I changed out of my robe and into some blue overalls—somewhat too large for me, but manageable—and some black, worn boots. I kept my hospital gown on underneath and rejoined Jack in front of the Kilns. Jack and Paxford were discussing the war.

"Ay, I think the Germans, ah, are ready for another raid, I'll wager," Paxford was saying. He seemed to use *ah* in more ways than I could count. "This one is sure to destroy London, y'll see. We'll all be speakin' German soon enough. 'Heil' this and 'heil' that." He raised his right hand in mock-ery of the Nazi salute.

"How cheery you are, Paxford," said Jack. "It can't be as bad as all that, can it?"

"I don't rightly know, Mr. Jack, but I do know we're at war—again—and that is never pleasant."

"Right you are, Paxford. Right you are." Jack saw me approaching. "Tom, I'm glad to see you back. Paxford, would you get the Daudel ready and bring it out, please?"

"Yes, sir. I'll do my best, but Major Lewis has driven it nearly into the ground, ye know. Won't be surprised if ye, ah, lose a tire on the way to London or get hit by a bus." Paxford, still muttering unpleasantries to himself, wandered off.

"Who is Major Lewis?" I asked.

"My brother, Warren."

For a few moments Jack seemed lost in thought. This gave me an op-portunity to survey my surroundings. I saw an inviting home of modest size, surrounded by foliage. The home seemed to have sprung up out of the earth, considering all the ivy growing on it. The white window frames stood out clearly against the red brick. I glimpsed a pond in the distance and, looking in another direction, saw two strange structures that looked almost like small pyramids, but each ending at their tips in large, cylindrical shapes. Jack must have noticed my puzzled expression.

"Those are the kilns—furnaces for baking bricks. Hence, the name of my home—The Kilns. We don't use them to make bricks, of course, but mainly for storage and such."

I nodded. "And why did you have Paxford build an air raid shelter?" I asked. I thought I noticed Jack blush slightly, which seemed out of character.

"Well, there was the war and the bombing, you know—the German blitz. For a time London suffered some serious attacks."

"Yes, but you are somewhat secluded here, aren't you? Isn't this near Oxford?"

Paxford's return interrupted our talk. "Ah, but Mr. Jack thought Hitler might have him singled out for attack—what with those broadcast talks of his, encouraging the nation and such. So I agreed to build the shelter. Not that I thought it'd do much good against German bombs."

As Paxford spoke, I saw he was walking a motorcycle in our direction. On its left side was a sidecar. *This*, I thought, *must be the Daudel.* The bike looked old—well-used and not necessarily in the best of shape.

"Is that—" I searched for the right word. "Safe?"

"I'm sure it's quite safe," replied Jack, though he looked doubtful.

"Of course it isn't safe!" said Paxford.

"I'm not sure I'll be comfortable riding in that little sidecar," I said.

"Good," said Jack, "because you'll be on the motorbike; I don't drive. Paxford, please give Tom some instructions on Daudel safety."

"Yes, Mr. Jack."

Despite my protests, in the end I was instructed briefly by Paxford in the basics of starting, stopping and steering. "Mind ye," warned Paxford, "ye might run into unexpected terrain or worse. Major Lewis wouldn't appreciate anything happenin' to his precious Daudel. And Mr. Jack, be careful. Ye don't look well. Feverish, I shouldn't wonder. Probably be, ah, flat on your back and in bed any day now. I'll prepare a chicken for some soup."

"Thank you, Paxford. I'm well enough. Are you ready, Tom?"

"I guess so," I said tentatively as I mounted the motorcycle. Jack reached into the sidecar for some goggles, which he put on. He stepped into the sidecar and, looking up at me, smiled broadly and appeared quite out of the ordinary, but game nonetheless.

"We may be back later, Paxford," said Jack. "Thanks again for your help."

"'Twas nothin' at all, Mr. Jack. Good to meet ye, Mr. Clerk."

"And you. Thanks again for the loan of the overalls and boots."

I started the Daudel, its engine noise breaking the serenity of the Kilns, and off we went. As we departed I thought I heard Paxford singing, somewhat off-key, "Abide with me, fast falls the eventide, the darkness deepens, Lord with me abide . . ."

"Where are we going?" I asked, as we picked up speed. The ride was bumpy, but not unbearable.

"London. I'll call out instructions as required," said Jack. I was surprised with how well I could hear him. I thought the noise of the motorcycle would be louder, but it appeared as though we would be able to continue our conversation while riding. Jack, at any rate, seemed eager to talk.

"It was in this sidecar that I came to believe that Jesus is the Son of God," he said, looking up at me, still wearing his goggles.

"I had no idea." It seemed a strange place for such a thing to occur.

"September 1931. We had planned an outing to Whipsnade Zoo. My brother had retreated to a room to read while the rest of us sorted out what he liked to call the 'kafuffle'—he meant 'kerfuffle'—wrangling over who would ride where. In the end I decided to ride with Warnie, in this very sidecar."

"And what happened on the way to the zoo? Did you have some kind of vision or something?"

"No, nothing like that. In fact, it was peaceful. I can't remember any specific emotion or directed thought pattern. I later compared the experience, in my book *Surprised by Joy,* to that of a man waking from a long sleep. Somehow, on the way to the zoo that morning, I realized I was spiritually awake. I had already converted to theism—a terrifying moment in my life, as God the hunter closed in—and now the next step seemed to take place quietly. There was no Damascus moment for me in this sidecar—no flash of light or voice of God like the apostle Paul received. And yet, by the time we arrived at the zoo, I realized that I had changed. Conversion and salvation, you know, are not always so neat and predictable as some Christians would like them to be."

"How so?" I asked, intrigued, but still concentrating on the road. Apparently my concentration was not good enough. Coming straight at me, at a rapid rate, I saw a large, golden double-decker bus on the wrong side of the road. *They're usually red,* I thought foolishly, a split second before reacting and realizing my mistake.

"Look out!" yelled Jack. "Left side! Left side of the road!" I swerved just in time.

"Sorry," I said sheepishly.

"No matter. We'll catch up with the bus later. Now, you were asking me about my comment regarding salvation and conversion not being so neat and predictable. That's the question, isn't it? What is it that makes a convert? What is conversion? And what is the relationship with salvation? Do you know that Augustine was moved by the voice of a child he overheard saying 'Pick it up and read' over and over again? Augustine took it as a sign and opened a manuscript—the book of Romans. Not long after, he believed in Christ. Me, I went through many 'isms' before arriving here in this sidecar—before believing in Christ."

"So is conversion an experience, a process or what?" I asked, genuinely curious.

"I think it is both—and probably more than we can fathom. My conversion was certainly a process, largely intellectual in my case. I moved through beliefs such as atheism and pantheism before converting to theism. Only later did my acceptance of Christ and Christianity come in. I would say that my conversion to theism in 1929 was the watershed moment, which is why I wrote about it so dramatically in *Surprised by Joy*. Some readers—those who aren't careful—have interpreted that section as referring to my becoming a Christian. If they read on to the beginning of the next chapter they will see that this was indeed a conversion to theism. In short, I came to believe, most reluctantly, in a personal God. But I had yet to embrace the incarnation—God's Son, Jesus Christ."

"I see. What would you call that experience then? Was it your conversion?"

"Not necessarily. It was part of the process on my way to becoming a Christian—a necessary step. Before one can believe in Christianity, one must believe a great many things. For instance, one must believe that God exists, is personal, is capable of performing miracles, has revealed himself to us, that logical and meaningful communication are real, that truth can be known and so forth. For the average atheist, if there is such a thing, most of Christianity is meaningless simply because Christian efforts to communicate make too many assumptions."

"I think you're right about that," I agreed.

"What I tried to do in the early portions of *Mere Christianity* was step back a few steps and try and reach people at an earlier stage, not assuming they were ready to hear and understand the gospel of Christ."

"And how did you do that?"

"We can speak more of that soon. For now, let us continue to explore the question of conversion."

"Fine. So after you became a theist what happened?"

"That will take too long to tell. I knew I had crossed an important threshold, and even though I was not a Christian, I did begin to attend church."

I glanced at Jack quizzically.

"Well, I felt I had to do something to 'show my colors' so to speak—to indicate that something had changed in me. I also began to read the Gospel of Saint John, in Greek mind you. I did not, by the way, see the Gospels as particularly great literature. To the literary critic in me they lacked the imagination and style of great myths and legends, which is one of the reasons I believed the Gospels to be genuine. Besides, the authors are quite blunt about revealing potentially embarrassing moments—places where the disciples often look like fools, for instance."

I admit I was intrigued. I had heard my share of Christian conversion stories in my day—testimonies, some called them—from Christians who had tried to convert me. Whenever they could not convince me by argument, and few even bothered to try, they would share their testimony—full of drama and feeling, but little intellectual rigor.

"And on the way to the zoo—in that sidecar—it just happened? You became a Christian?"

"Yes, but it's odd that I don't really recall anything particularly profound about the experience. It was two years after my conversion to theism so I don't believe I rushed into anything based, for instance, merely on emotion. In fact, I don't recall feeling particularly emotional. There was no blinding light or vision or such, as I said. It just made sense to take the next step."

"And how old were you?"

"I don't think that matters much, but in my case I was about your age, I'd guess—just a couple of months short of my thirty-third year."

"And was there a change in you—say, in your character?"

"That generally accompanies Christian conversion, or at least it should if the conversion is genuine. In my case I think there was a change, but I think it was gradual. One of my favorite characters in my Narnia stories, named Eustace Clarence Scrubb—and he almost deserved it!—goes through something of a conversion process in *The Voyage of the 'Dawn Treader.'*"

"I don't think I've read that one. I would have remembered a name like Eustace Clarence."

"In the book, Eustace is a prig—quarrelsome, troublemaking and just plain nasty. Because of his greed, he is transformed into a dragon. It is during this dragonish period that he begins to change—to become a better individual. After he is 'undragoned' by Aslan the lion, Eustace starts to become a better person. It is not instantaneous, by any means. He, like any convert, had his relapses, but on the whole he had begun to be cured."

"And how is Eustace 'undragoned'?"

"Aslan throws him into a pool and instructs Eustace to remove his skin—to shed like a snake. Eustace does this three times, but still the skin remains. It is up to Aslan to remove the boy's skin—and it hurts. It is much thicker than Eustace had ever anticipated."

"So the water is a metaphor for baptism, while the lion stands for God? And only God can remove our thick, dragon skin in order to change us for the better?"

"I prefer not to say too much about the interpretation of my stories," said Jack. I took a moment to glance down at him. He wore, in addition to his goggles, a sly grin.

"And what of salvation? How does that relate to conversion?"

"Conversion, I think, results in salvation. By salvation God grants deliverance from the power and hold of sin in our lives through what Christ has done for us. This deliverance, however, is a process, too. Every day we are presented with choices. Our reactions to those choices—both small and great—move us more toward God and virtue or more in the other direction—to vice and all that comes with it. Over the course of a lifetime all of these choices combine to either make us creatures who are more heavenly or more hellish."

"Is salvation permanent, then?"

"That depends on what type of Christian you ask. As you may know, I prefer to stay within the bounds of 'mere Christianity' as much as possible and avoid emphasis on disagreements between Christians. If a soul can be reclaimed by the enemy—and I say 'if'—then, in the end, I believe it is so because of our own choices."

"And what is 'mere Christianity'?"

"Many people think it originated with me, but they are greatly mistaken! Most of my ideas, in fact, are merely popularizations of the ideas of great thinkers who came before me. Mere Christianity I got from Richard Baxter who wrote, in part, in 1680, 'I am a Christian, a Mere Christian, of no other Religion; and the Church that I am of is the Christian Church. . . . But must you know what Sect or Party I am of? I am against all Sects and dividing Parties.' Mere Christianity is what all Christians throughout the ages have believed in—the core beliefs. The resurrection, the deity of our Lord Jesus Christ, the reality of sin and the need for human redemption by God's grace, and so forth."

"Do you expect to make me a Christian with mere Christianity?"

"I do not expect to 'make you' anything. That is up to you. But, seeing that you are an atheist, I think you have some time ahead of you before you come around, assuming you do. I can only offer you reasons and evidence for belief, but it is up to you, in the end, to believe or not. God will let you make your choice, however unfortunate that may end up being for you in the end."

I noticed the countryside had changed significantly. Ahead of us, not too distant, I saw a great city.

"London," said Jack.

7

A Mere Christian on the Air

In which we dodge bombs, visit the BBC studios, discuss "mere" Christianity and debate about Jesus.

We were quiet for a time, as I contemplated Jack's conversion story. All too soon, however, the silence broke. Now in London, making our way to the BBC, as Jack explained, the world around me began to shatter with sounds I had only imagined or heard in films. Air-raid sirens blared. The earth shook, momentarily causing the motorbike to swerve. I began to slow down.

"Are you mad?" screamed Jack. "It's a blitz—can't you see the planes?" He pointed up.

"What do you mean?"

"The Germans are attacking! Get us out of here."

I glanced up and saw countless silhouettes of planes, many of them dropping large objects—bombs, I surmised. My heart raced and we sped away, with Jack shouting directions. By the time we arrived at the BBC, the planes were gone, leaving behind rubble, fear, and also, Jack told me, determination.

Eager to leave the motorcycle behind in exchange for more formidable shelter, I parked in front of the BBC. Jack got out of the sidecar, leaving his goggles behind, and together we entered the building. The front desk loomed before us, unoccupied. In fact, we saw no one in the building.

"Where is everyone?" I asked.

"I don't know. It suits our purposes, however. Follow me to the recording studio."

"What recording studio?"

"Where I gave my broadcast talks—the ones that were later turned into the book *Mere Christianity.*"

Jack seemed to know the way easily. We made two brief stops, near one office with a plaque outside that read "Dr. James Welch" and another that belonged to an Eric Fenn. Welch, explained Jack, served as director of religious broadcasting for the BBC and had contacted Jack in 1941, asking if he would be interested in being on the air. Fenn served as assistant head of religious broadcasting and, as a result, had also interacted with Jack extensively.

As he explained this, we heard a voice, apparently coming from Welch's office. Jack opened the door and entered. I glanced around the room and saw a desk covered with papers, a worn copy of Lewis's book *The Problem of Pain,* some photographs, a chair, a rotary phone, an old radio and a well-used typewriter.

"Hello? Is anyone there?" said a deep, rich voice, broken with intermittent static, coming from the radio. Thinking it was a radio program, I reached over to turn it off.

"Wait," said Jack.

"What is it?"

"Hello?" said the radio voice again.

"I know that voice—on the wireless," Jack said.

"Jack, is that you?" the voice continued. "It's James—James Welch."

"Radios don't usually work this way," I whispered to Jack.

"No, they don't," Jack replied, looking puzzled.

"James, so good to hear from you," Jack said to the radio. "But why didn't you just use the telephone?"

"This seemed more convenient, especially considering that you have a guest with you, don't you?"

"Yes, I do. This is Thomas Clerk with me, James." Even though Welch could not see us, Jack gestured to me with a hand, as he stooped over the desk, his face close to the radio.

"Welcome to the British Broadcasting Corporation, Mr. Clerk."

"Thank you," I said.

"Jack, the bombing seems to have stopped for now, but do be careful." Static interfered, causing Welch's voice to break up slightly.

"We'll be careful, James," answered Jack.

"Pleasure to speak with you, Mr. Clerk. Has Jack told you all about how he ended up on our airwaves?"

"Not quite," I said.

"What did I originally ask you to speak about, Jack?"

"Christianity and modern literature, I think."

"Yes, that's right! Jack politely declined. But my second suggestion caught his attention—your views of the Christian faith based on your unique perspectives as a layman and former atheist."

"Correct," said Jack. "I wrote back to you asking to speak about the law of nature—the objectivity of right and wrong."

"It was a stroke of genius to begin the talks that way, I think," said Welch. "Your concern, as I remember, was the fact that too many people were not ready to hear the message of Christianity—namely, the need for repentance—because they had no real knowledge of this natural law—of absolute moral standards rooted in God. In that respect, they were quite different from the New Testament audience."

"Quite right. The audience addressed by Jesus, primarily first-century Hebrews, accepted the reality of the existence of God, as well as the reality of an absolute standard of morality—a standard they knew, in most cases, that they could not keep."

"I see," I said, noncommittally. "And how did you come to select Jack for this project?"

"What was it? Oh, I remember," spoke Welch, a bit of static interfering again. "I had read *The Problem of Pain* and found it most edifying—personally and intellectually. It's a fine book."

"Thank you, James," Jack said.

"You're welcome, as always. And do enjoy your visit, Mr. Clerk. Goodbye, Jack."

"Goodbye."

The static on the radio crackled a bit, broken seconds later by the sounds of big band music.

We left the office and, with Jack leading the way, made our way to a recording studio. To my modern eyes used to advanced computer technology, the BBC equipment looked as I expected—antiquated. And yet it intrigued me. Dials, knobs, a small area separated by glass, presumably for those working on broadcasts behind the scenes. Nothing digital or computerized. On the wall inside the studio hung a simple analog clock. I saw a large microphone marked "BBC" on a table. Jack sat in one of the two chairs near the table, motioning me to sit in the other one.

"How far have you gotten in my book?" said Jack.

A bit embarrassed that I had not read more, I answered, "I've only started on the preface."

"Good!" Jack said. "In that case we can review some of the material in the first section, then. The first set of broadcast talks was promoted as 'Right and Wrong: A Clue to the Meaning of the Universe.'"

"So you presented a moral argument for the existence of God?"

"Yes, that's right."

"This should be interesting. I've read about moral arguments for God and have found them unconvincing."

"Humor me," said Jack.

"Okay."

"You have heard people arguing?"

"Yes, of course."

"And when people argue, what is their purpose?"

"Usually there is some conflict between the parties and each side is trying to show that the other side is wrong and that they are right."

"Exactly. Would you say, then, that the arguers are appealing to some kind of standard and that they expect one another to adhere to this standard?"

"That depends on the kind of argument they are having, I guess." I had a pretty good idea, I thought, of where Jack was heading with this argument, but that didn't mean I was going to make it easy for him.

"Let's say that you were waiting in line to see a play," continued Jack, "and as you turned your back for a moment, I suddenly cut in front of you along with a group of several of my friends."

"I'd say that would be wrong."

"And what if I disagreed?"

"Then we would have an argument."

"Correct. The argument, however, involves an appeal to a certain kind of behavior that people expect from one another. It's not fair for me and my friends to cut in line in front of you. In baseball, for example, there would be no point in saying a ball was a foul unless rules of baseball were agreed upon and established. My point is that a standard of behavior needs to exist beyond an argument so that the standard can be appealed to. This standard is what people have called the law of nature, the law of human nature or natural law."

"I think you're making quite a leap to come to that conclusion so quickly. How do you know this 'standard,' as you call it, is natural law?" I said. "And if it is, how do you get to God from this line of reasoning?"

"Well, if you mean the God of Christianity, then I agree that my argument thus far does not directly support the existence of the biblical God. Rather, I'm trying to take things in steps. You, I think, will agree that before someone can come to believe in Christianity, one must first believe that God exists?"

"That makes sense."

"I think so too. One of the things I tried to accomplish with my version of a moral argument for God was that, on the basis of the reality of a moral law, something exists that is more like mind—more personal—than not. This something gave us this law, placed it within us, one could say. After all, one cannot have moral law without a moral lawgiver."

"I think we can," I objected. "What you call natural law might just be social convention—we follow the 'rules' because society needs to function in an orderly manner. It could also be purely biological—survival instinct and such. A Darwinian model could support what we perceive as moral standards, which are in reality nothing but evolutionary leftovers or survival instinct."

"I disagree. Moral law stipulates standards of personal action between personal beings. In your 'Darwinian' model, as you put it, though you would agree that personality exists, I don't think you have a good explanation for it. All is random chance mixed with time. There is no personal guide involved. Everything must happen, on your own grounds, on its own and by chance. But can a random, impersonal universe somehow produce standards that dictate personal interaction between personal beings? That seems a stretch."

"I still think it's possible. I also think you're jumping ahead of yourself. I don't agree that you have established that these moral standards really exist, much less that they are grounded in something resembling a god."

"Yes, I think I have jumped ahead," said Jack. "In my first broadcast talks I made the case for the reality of moral law. I did this because I believed that most Christian efforts to defend and make the case for Christianity—apologetics—assumed too much prior knowledge. Before Christianity makes real sense, one must of course believe that God exists, but there must also be a sense of guilt over the breaking of moral law. Otherwise, the Christian gospel makes no sense. It calls men and women to repentance, but surely before there can be a reaction there must be a realization that repentance is needed. In the first century—the audience of Christ's time—they understood the reality of moral law. Not so in the 1940s, nor in your day."

"So you were not trying to proselytize or evangelize?"

"I did not see it that way, no. What I was doing was more along the lines of what some might consider 'pre-evangelism.' As a former atheist, I tried to craft arguments that would move people along in the direction of Christianity through reasoned arguments, not impassioned sermons. Besides, being limited by the time constraints of radio, every phrase had to count. So when I began I attempted to demonstrate first, that a moral law exists and calls us to act in a certain way and, second, that we break this law. In these early talks I also attempted to demonstrate that without absolute moral law, there is no room for moral criticism, at least not logically, even in cases where such criticism is clearly warranted, such as when declaring Nazi morality to be wrong."

I had heard variations of this argument before. Given the atrocities committed by the Nazi regime, atheists were said to have no grounds for opposing such behavior.

"But couldn't such behavior—Nazi morality, as you call it," I countered, "be condemned on the basis of the judgment of humanity?"

"But judgment based on what, Tom? With anthropologists laying the groundwork for cultural relativism, truth and moral standards are made out to be cultural. If this is true—somewhat of a paradox in and of itself—then we had no business telling the Germans they were wrong. Exterminating six million Jews was, on such grounds, merely part of their cultural mandate. Who were we to interfere? But on the basis of moral law, we had no choice but to interfere. Evil must be overcome, lest the world enter into utter darkness."

"You're assuming that I don't believe in morality, but I do."

"Yes, I know that. My point is that you may believe in it, indeed you must believe because it is written on your heart as well as mine, as Saint Paul writes in the second chapter of his Epistle to the Romans, but you have no real foundation for it. You cut off your foundation when you dispense with God. It is as though you are sitting on a limb, rebelling against the tree it is attached to, all the while going about your business of sawing off the limb you are sitting on."

"I don't see it that way."

"Of course you don't. As a committed atheist, to see it that way would grant the reality of God, and your entire belief structure—your *Weltanschauung* or worldview—would eventually come crashing down. It's not an easy step to take. Believe me, I know. The question, however, is not whether or not it is an easy step to take, but whether or not it is true."

"Obviously, you think it is true. I don't."

"I do. Ideas such as justice and loyalty demand that it be true. Without a transcendent moral law, given by a transcendent moral lawgiver, any attempts at ethics on our part will, like it or not, degenerate into chaos. That is why, I think, you find yourself in your day facing the kinds of ethical issues you are facing. Why shouldn't a scientist experiment, whatever the methods, in order to further progress? Why shouldn't eugenicists—genetic engineers—do what is necessary to further human knowledge? And, some day, why shouldn't some rule over others and even experiment on them for the 'greater good' of scientific progress? In the end you will have *The Island of Doctor Moreau*, perhaps not as vividly gone wrong as in the H. G. Wells book, but something much like it. Whatever it is called, it will lead, if left unchecked, to the destruction of the human race. Stepping beyond God's moral standards, you step into nothing."

"We've been over that, Jack. I think you are on a slippery slope, exaggerating what you think might happen. I don't think it will. But getting back to your earlier point, you claim that absolute moral law requires a moral lawgiver—what you believe to be God?"

"Yes, that's right."

"Don't you have a problem?"

"How so?"

"As I see it, this moral law is either just declared by God to be so, making it appear arbitrary, or God is merely appealing to some moral standard that is beyond him, making him appear unnecessary—superfluous."

"Ah, yes, the Euthyphro dilemma. I applaud your succinct presentation of Plato's argument—or the argument of Socrates as presented by his pupil, if one takes that approach," said Jack. "I addressed this somewhat in my essay 'The Poison of Subjectivism.'"

I should have guessed. Was there anything Jack did not discuss somewhere?

"The way Socrates sets it forth in the dialogue," Jack added, "is as follows, 'Is the pious loved by the gods because it is pious, or is it pious because it is loved by the gods?' The point being, as you summarized, that, according to this dialogue, either God merely declares things good or he appeals to something beyond himself that is the source of what is good. Both horns of the Euthyphro dilemma are intolerable. But that is the problem with dilemma—it commits the logical error of offering false alternatives. There could be a third way, another solution, a *tertium quid*, to use philosophical language. God, you see, is by his very nature, goodness. God is goodness and goodness is God. Morality, then is neither arbitrary nor beyond God. Instead, it is rooted in his very nature. Since God does not change, neither do his ethical standards."

"You are passionate, Jack, but I am unconvinced. Why don't you think our seeming reactions or behavior in response to 'moral law' is not simply instinctive?"

"Herd instinct, you mean? Since supposedly instinctual responses are sometimes in conflict, but we sometimes give in to the weaker instinct or impulse, it is reasonable to conclude that herd instinct is not a valid explanation of universal moral law. If it were, then we would always obey the stronger impulse, but we do not always do so. When two instincts or impulses are in conflict, there is actually a third force at work—something that judges and decides between the two impulses. This third thing cannot be either of the other two. In reality, it is moral law pressing upon us to aid us in making the right choice."

"Again, this seems like sleight of hand to me," I said. "How can you know there is a third force at work? How can you prove it is not merely biological instinct?"

"I didn't say I could prove my point with 100 percent certainty. My point about herd instinct is one of many points I make in support of moral law. It is really a response to one of several objections to my argument. Another is social convention, which you mentioned earlier."

"If you mean by social convention that we are indoctrinated, so to speak, into buying into moral law, then I think I agree. It is our social environment, our cultural upbringing and education that hammer into us this moral law."

"And if that is the case," said Jack, "then what is your explanation for it?"

"This makes morality merely human tradition," I replied. "Take a child from birth and teach him or her what you believe is right and wrong and of course most such children will grow up believing in right and wrong, moral law and the rest of it. They are haunted by the blunders of their parents."

"What do you mean by 'haunted'?" asked Jack.

"I mean that the mistakes of previous generations, their blind stumblings in a universe without God, results in what you call 'morality' being passed on from one generation to the next. It is the atheists—in the minority, I agree—who break away from their social and moral conditioning and see reality as it truly is."

"And what they end up seeing is bleak. Even Bertrand Russell, hero to many atheists, realized that. What was it that he wrote in his essay 'A Free Man's Worship'? 'Brief and powerless is Man's life; on him and all his race the slow, sure doom falls pitiless and dark. Blind to good and evil, reckless of destruction, omnipotent matter rolls on its relentless way; for Man, condemned today to lose his dearest, tomorrow himself to pass through the gate of darkness.' What a cheery man! At least Russell had the courage to acknowledge where his unbelief would logically lead—a meaningless universe with no hope for anyone. Of course, on his view there is no grounding for courage. Again, I return us to the question of truth. If atheism is true, then by all means let us face it and embrace it, however grim the outcome. But if it is not, then we must know the truth. Social conditioning will not allow you to escape moral law."

"Why not?"

"Merely because we are taught something does not mean that the something in question is merely human invention. Would this be the case in mathematics? Is the solution to two plus two only four because society has conditioned us to accept this or are mathematical solutions true regardless of our conditioning? I agree that we learn moral laws from others. Some of what we learn is mere social convention, but other things we learn are like mathematical truths—they are rooted in the reality of moral law that everyone knows. That, in fact, is why we are taught these truths—because everyone, deep down inside, knows them. My question is, who put them there? In my assessment, the director or power behind this moral law is God."

"And that is supposed to prove Christianity to me?"

"No! I admit that I am still quite a ways from making that case. What my argument from morality is supposed to demonstrate is that something exists that is more like mind—more personal—than it is not. This mind has an interest in right and wrong and, as such, has ingrained this into our very being. If such a being is not God—or very much like God—then I don't know what else to call it. But this argument merely paves the way for the reality of the Christian God."

"And you think you succeeded?"

"I think if the evidence is looked at fairly the argument has some merit. It does not attempt to shatter all obstacles to this goal. You seem to want one argument that will prove Christianity, when in reality there are several lines of reasoning making the case for Christian truth. What I am also trying to demonstrate is that we can get quite far on our own steam. I have not appealed to the Bible or the words of Christ with my moral argument—what theologians call 'special revelation.'"

"Then what does your moral law argument offer?" I asked, still skeptical.

"The moral law is a clue—a very big one—to the solution to ultimate reality. But repentance and the need for forgiveness, two important Christian points, make no real sense unless one faces the reality of moral law and the fact that something exists that is behind it. If the reality of moral law is granted, or if at least someone is made open to this possibility, then we are not too far from acknowledging that there is a power behind this law. And if we routinely break this law, then that tells us that we are likely out of favor with this power. It is at this stage that the Christian message may make some progress."

"That still leaves a lot of questions unanswered," I said.

"Yes, I realize that it is not a perfect argument," said Jack. "Some may come away from it and become deists, believing in a distant God who has nothing to do with day-to-day realities of our existence. Others may come to believe in a limited god—one who lacks power to deal with evil, for instance. Still others may realize that they have been breaking these moral standards for years, leading them to despair. That is where Christianity comes in to offer real hope."

"And others might just reject your argument outright," I muttered. I had heard moral arguments before. The danger to the atheist, of course, is that of granting the reality of moral law rooted in some kind of transcendent personality. If the argument is successful, then the atheist has something that must be addressed—a dilemma involving what many would argue is something that exists that is, if not God, then very like God. To escape the dilemma, an atheist must reject the reality of a transcendent moral standard, but not necessarily jettison morality. Morality simply must be established on grounds other than theism. Jack had talked some sense, but my atheism was holding steady.

"You said that Christianity offers hope," I said, "but it only offers hope if it's true. I don't see how that can be determined."

"It all comes down to what one does with the person of Christ," Jack continued. "He himself posed the question to his disciples—'Who do you say that I am?' The answer to this question is key."

"And obviously your solution to the question is that Christ is God?"

"Naturally. But I think it only fair to present the options, which is what I did on my broadcast talks. The 'shocking alternative' that I came up with was that Christ is who he claimed to be—God incarnate. All other explanations fall short."

"And what, in your opinion, are the options?"

"Opinion? I have no opinion on this matter. It is a matter of logic."

He was again starting to sound like Kirkpatrick; I'd have to be cautious.

"It is clear from the New Testament that Christ claimed to be God," said Jack.

"Is it?"

"If one takes the time to read it in context, then, yes, I think it is clear."

"Can you point to a passage where Jesus declares he is God?"

"I don't think he was quite that transparent in his presentation of his claims to deity, at least not to modern readers. If you press the point, however, I think his dialogue with the Jews in the eighth chapter of the Gospel of Saint John is fairly clear. Christ claimed in verse fifty-six that Abraham rejoiced to see his day. The Jews retorted in the next verse that Jesus wasn't even fifty years old, yet he claimed to have seen Abraham. Jesus replied by saying, 'Verily, verily, I say unto you, Before Abraham was, I am.' In saying 'I am,' Christ used the exact words of the Greek translation of the Old Testament—the Septuagint—*egō eimi*—that were used in Exodus 3:14 wherein God gives his name to Moses. The Jews understood this as a claim to deity. In fact, in another passage the Jews picked up stones to stone him for making himself out to be God."

"Even if what you say is true, Jesus did not say, 'I am God.'"

"You're missing the point, Tom. Jesus gave many indications of deity. The passage in John is merely one of them. He also claimed the capacity to forgive sins."

"What's the big deal with that? I don't see how it makes him God. I can forgive, too."

"Let me elaborate," said Jack. "In the particular passage I have in mind—Luke 5:20—a crippled man is lowered through the ceiling of a home. Jesus proceeds to tell the man that his sins are forgiven. Now, if I happen to step on your toe, it would be quite natural for you, being gracious, to forgive me. But what if a third party entered the room and, before we could discuss the matter of the injured toe, this person said to me, 'I forgive you for stepping on Tom's toe.' Doesn't that strike you as odd? Yet that is what Christ did, from a human perspective. The Jews of his day, however, once again interpreted his actions and words clearly. In Luke 5:21 they asked, 'Who can forgive sins but God alone?'"

Clearly I was not going to beat Jack at a game of Bible-thumping. I would have to take a different approach.

"Let me, then, for the sake of argument," I said, "agree that the Bible teaches that Christ claimed to be God. Who is to say that it is reliable? Isn't it possible that his followers changed the story, so to speak, and either invented Christ altogether or embellished his story?"

"That would be the mythology or legend option, Tom. I regret that time did not allow me to address that alternative in my broadcast talks. Given my earthly profession—my knowledge of literature, myth and legend—I can tell you that the Gospels do not read as legend or myth. I'm sorry to say that as far as quality myths are concerned, the New Testament writers would come off as clumsy by comparison to other mythological literature. They simply do not have the flavor of legend or myth.

Besides, some portions of the New Testament, as even liberal scholars agree, were written within two decades of the death of Christ. There is no time for legends to form. Many who were alive during the time of Christ would have protested—many of them loudly—over the supposedly false claims made in the Gospels. Yet they did not."

"But the church could have tampered with the manuscripts at a later date."

"The manuscript evidence does not support that theory. The New Testament is incredibly reliable."

"So, in your opinion—I mean, according to your conclusions—Christ claimed to be Lord and you reject the option that he is legend?"

"Correct. But I grant that it is possible that he could have been a liar or a madman. Based on what we know of him, I find it quite a stretch to consider that he may have been a liar."

"Why?"

"Why, on the basis of his character—his ethical teachings. Even atheists—those who don't deny the reality of the historical Jesus—grant that his moral standards are worth attention. It was not in his character to lie. Quite the opposite. He was the one who would often preface his remarks with 'Verily, verily,' or in more recent translations, 'I tell you the truth.' Jesus was no liar. He came to 'bear witness unto the truth,' as he himself said."

"And couldn't he have been a lunatic?"

"Find me a reputable scholar who would agree with you, on the basis of the evidence and a viable interpretation of the New Testament."

"I heard that Albert Schweitzer believed Jesus was mentally disturbed."

"I think you are referring to his book *The Psychiatric Study of Jesus.*"

"I'm not sure." Again, Jack was one step ahead of my objection.

"Schweitzer reads into the biblical text what is not there in order to come to his conclusions. He claims incidents such as Jesus cleansing the temple by toppling tables and using a whip of chords demonstrate his emotional instability, as do incidents such as the withering of the fig tree. Schweitzer has to do some creative interpretation indeed in order to conclude from such incidents that Jesus was insane. Looking at the overall picture one gets of Christ from a straightforward reading of the Gospels, one does not come away thinking that Christ was deranged. So, then, Christ was no liar, neither was he legend, neither was he a lunatic. And yet he claimed to be Lord. The argument I sketched along these lines in my broadcast talks was brief, but I think we have covered the basics."

"But couldn't Christ have merely been a man—surely a great man, but why not the option that he was merely human?"

"And I am a poached egg!" Jack laughed. "If I said that, with no evidence backing my claim, and took it seriously, then I would be mad. A person who said and did the kinds of things you find Jesus saying and doing is no ordinary man. Besides, the biblical record is clear that he claimed to be Lord, so we are back again to my options. Christ proved his claims by not only predicting his death and resurrection, but by actually rising from the grave."

"I don't know. You make it seem too neat, as though the options you provide are the only ones or, at any rate, you seem to stack the deck in your favor."

"Then give me an answer to who Christ was—an answer that stands up under rational scrutiny, biblical and historical evidence—and I am prepared to listen." He leaned back a bit in his chair.

"I don't hold this position, but I've heard some say that Jesus traveled East and learned what he did from gurus. Maybe Jesus was just a guru?" I didn't want it to come out this way, but it sounded more like a question than an answer. I admit that I was grasping at straws at this point. I did not believe Jack's logic was as ironclad as he made it out to be, but I was not as quick on my feet, mentally speaking, as he was.

"It sounds as though you don't even believe that one, Tom. To say that Jesus was merely claiming to be God because he learned it from the East is to completely disregard the context of the New Testament. We are dealing with first-century Jews, for the most part. They believed in one, personal, transcendent God. In short, they were theists. Jesus never taught that everyone was part of the divine—pantheism. He was a theist. The options remain. The best solution is that Christ was and is who he claimed to be. What you do with that knowledge is up to you."

Jack looked at the clock on the wall. "Oh dear, it's time to go! We don't want to be late."

"Where are we going now?" I asked.

"Somewhere else, of course," said Jack with a smile. He stood up and we exited the studio.

"Let's take the lift this time," he said, referring to an elevator we were approaching. I pressed the down button and we waited. When the doors opened, we stepped in. Jack pressed two numbers, 4 and 9, even though I did not think the building had nine levels. We began to descend, then I felt a noticeable shift.

"Are we moving sideways?"

"It's possible," said Jack. "We have a ways to go."

The doors opened to a night sky and a road lined with streetlights.

"There it is," Jack said, pointing to a building. I glanced in the direction Jack indicated and saw a building with a sign hanging in front of it that read "Eagle and Child."

8

Friends at the Pub

Wherein we visit a pub, but beer eludes me, and we have a discussion with the Inklings about love, friendship and reason.

"Here we are, 49 St. Giles, Oxford," said Jack. *That explained the 4 and 9 in the elevator,* I thought.

I looked up at a rectangular sign. The rich, blue background accentuated the main emphasis of the portrait—a magnificent brown eagle carrying a baby. Below the portrait were the words "Eagle and Child."

"We called it the Bird and Baby," said Jack. "I'm not quite sure how old the building is, but it's been an inn since the seventeenth century—1650, as I recall. I met here regularly, every Tuesday, with a group of friends who became known as the Inklings. In fact, we met here for more than twenty years. In 1962 we decided to move our meeting to the Lamb and Flag pub across the street," Jack said as he pointed to another building in the distance. "But for more than two decades, the Bird and Baby was our most regular meeting place."

The building itself was unremarkable. The unassuming entranceway featured a single door leading into the public house. Jack explained that a public house or 'pub' was not really like what Americans considered a bar, but more of a restaurant or friendly gathering place. On either side of the door were identical windows—white, rectangular frames, with each window divided vertically in two. The bottom portion of the front entrance, perhaps about three feet from the bottom to about the middle of the door, was painted black, while the rest of the building was a sort of beige color, though it was a bit difficult to make out in the dark.

"Let's go inside, shall we?" Jack said as he opened the door.

The simple entrance consisted of a bar area with several stools, which got me thinking that I'd enjoy a cold beer despite my doctor's protests, but I had little time to examine this area, as Jack quickly moved on. We made our way to a back room—Jack called it a parlor—which he dubbed "The Rabbit Room." A small fire heated the room, though not very well. Inside the parlor were three men, one of whom I recognized as J. R. R. Tolkien. He was the first to notice us enter and caught Jack's eye.

"Tollers!" Jack said as he heartily offered a greeting, nearly knocking the pipe from Tolkien's mouth in the process.

"Jack," Tolkien said, greeting him with a smile. "It's so good to see you again. And Tom," he said, pausing briefly, perhaps taking in my oversized overalls, "I'm glad to see you again as well."

A large man sitting in a corner took what looked like a last drink from his mug, stood and came over to us.

"Warnie, I'm glad you could join us," said Jack.

"You know I wouldn't miss an opportunity to visit the Bird and Baby," said Jack's brother, Warren Lewis. "Is the Daudel still in one piece?"

"Yes, Warnie, it's fine," said Jack, adding with, I thought, an expression of mock seriousness, "although we almost hit a bus and were bombed in London."

Jack's brother frowned. "And who do we have here?" he asked, gesturing to me.

"Warnie, this is Tom. We've been traveling together for some time now.

Tom, this is my brother, Major Warren Lewis." Warnie nodded in my direction.

The third man, still seated at a table, was writing feverishly in a note-pad. He looked thin, had a mop of disheveled dark hair and wore glasses with dark rounded frames. An air of intensity fluttered about him. Jack took a seat opposite the man with the notebook, while I sat next to Jack. Tolkien sat next to the writing man, and Warnie found a spot at the end of the table.

"Charles!" bellowed Jack as he slammed a fist on the table near the notepad. Though I was startled, the writing man merely paused and looked up, as though he was already aware of new arrivals in the parlor.

"Hello, Jack," said the man quietly.

"Tom, let me introduce you to C. W.—Charles Williams, that is. Charles, this is Tom Clerk." We shook hands.

Tolkien interrupted the greeting. "What is it tonight, Jack, the usual business of the Inklings?"

"What's your 'usual business'? And what are the Inklings?" I asked, speaking for the first time since our greeting.

"I'd hardly call it 'business,'" said Jack. "We weren't that organized. Mostly we Inklings just got together for friendship and to read and dis-cuss projects we were working on. Tollers here read many a draft from *The Lord of the Rings,* Warnie read excerpts from his historical works on seven-teenth-century France, and C. W. read from some of his writings."

Charles Williams and his writings were not familiar to me. Jack must have interpreted that based on my expression, so he continued.

"Charles, of course, also wrote some fine works—"

"'Supernatural thrillers'—isn't that what T. S. Eliot called them?" said Warnie.

"Yes, supernatural thrillers. *War in Heaven, All Hallow's Eve, Descent Into*

Hell and so forth. My personal favorite for a time was *The Place of the Lion.*" Williams smiled slightly and seemed to blush at Jack's compliment.

"And you read some of your works, too, Jack?" I asked.

"That he did," said Tolkien. He was about to light a match, presumably for use on the pipe he was holding in his hand. "What was the first big project you did as a result of the Inklings, Jack? *The Problem of Pain*, wasn't it?"

"Yes, I think so."

"He dedicated it to us, remember?" Warnie said.

"Hold on one moment," said Jack, looking at me. Suddenly everyone in the room stopped moving except for myself and Jack. Tolkien had struck his match, but the smoke hung in the air, unmoving. The flame, too, paused, like a photograph. Williams held two of his fingers to the frame of his glasses, just above his nose, apparently in the process of adjusting them, while Warren's right hand was extended, a single finger pointing at Tolkien.

"What's happened?" I asked, somewhat startled.

"Sometimes it takes years to get to know someone," said Jack. "In other cases less time is required, of course, but I thought a brief pause would help you learn just a bit more about my friends. Tolkien you've met earlier. You've indicated your familiarity with *The Lord of the Rings*, but Tolkien was much more than a writer of fantasy literature. He was born in South Africa in 1892, six years before I entered this world. Like myself, he fought in the Great War. A man fascinated by language and myth, he's quite a remarkable fellow. I first met him in 1926—at Oxford. I believe I made some comment in my diary after first meeting Tollers about him not being a bad fellow and just needing a smack or two." Jack laughed.

"And what about him?" I asked, gesturing to Williams.

"Charles is a different sort," said Jack, looking at Williams, still frozen in time, his fingers on the frame of his glasses, "yet the same in some ways. We all loved stories, and Charles, in that regard, fit in quite well. An editor with Oxford University Press for decades, he was not what you'd call scholarly in the sense of holding degrees and such, but I must say he was very well read and despite his common appearance could be quite charming. I owe a great debt to his influence on my writing, especially *That Hideous Strength.* One could call that book my first, and perhaps only, 'supernatural thriller.' Born in 1886, Charles beat both myself and Tollers into this world. Unfortunately, he beat us out of this life, too. In 1945, quite unexpectedly, he died. It was not my first great loss in life, but it struck me hard all the same . . ."

Jack paused a moment, startling me in the process, actually. You see, for a second I thought that perhaps he had now become a statue like the others. What would I do if Jack also froze in time?

"And then there is Warnie," said Jack, looking at his brother, seated at the table, still pointing a motionless finger at Tolkien. "My brother and friend. A soldier and a scholar, but also troubled with alcohol. I owe him much, too, of course. As boys we created an imaginary world—Animal-Land, which included a place called Boxen and, of all things, India. Talking animals and political intrigue ruled the day in Animal-Land. It was Warnie who showed me the toy garden so many years ago that caused a stirring in my soul—a stirring of longing and desire for joy that eluded me for so many years. Well, then, let's get back to the conversation, shall we?"

"Yes, of course," I said. In an instant everyone was moving again. Tolkien's match had gone out before he had a chance to light his pipe, Williams completed adjusting his glasses, and Warren lowered his finger.

"Quite right, quite right—it was *The Problem of Pain* that Jack dedicated to the Inklings," Tolkien said.

"What are we here for, Jack?" asked Williams in a subdued tone.

"We're here for Tom," said Jack, glancing at me as he spoke.

"Are we supposed to do something for him? Oh, please don't tell me he's a budding writer and he's brought a thick manuscript for us to critique!" blurted Tolkien with a chuckle.

"No, none of that! We just need to talk, I think."

"That's easy enough," said Williams, "but what shall we talk about?" He gently pressed his glasses onto his nose and looked at me with his strange intensity. They all looked.

"Since you all seem such good friends, maybe you could tell me about that," I suggested, not really knowing what to say. The topic seemed safe enough, though knowing Jack he would somehow bring it around to my spiritual condition and the ultimate questions of life.

"Oh that will get Jack started," said Tolkien. *"The Four Loves* and all that."

"What are the four loves?" I inquired.

"*Storgē, philia, erōs* and *agapē*, of course," said Tolkien, jabbing his unlit pipe in the air as he said each word.

"You might want to expand that a bit for the sake of our guest, professor," said Williams.

"Actually," I said, "I've heard at least some of those words before, though I don't claim expertise on any of them."

Tolkien stood up and paced the parlor briefly, then began.

"You see, Jack gave some radio talks on the four loves—he was quite the radio personality, you know—and later wrote a book called *The Four Loves,* wherein he explored four Greek words for love: *storgē, philia, erōs* and *agapē*. Friendship, you see, is one of the four loves: *philia*."

"I think," said Williams, "that we should make a point of distinguishing *philia* from superficial friendships, if one can even call such relationships 'friendships.'"

"Hear, hear!" said Warren.

"When I speak of friendship in the *philia* sense," said Jack, "I mean a true friendship—one that endures, one that sees friends enjoying one another's company as they pursue common interests, one that lasts despite areas of disagreement. I believe there are two primary reasons why *philia* is often misunderstood. First, I don't think many people actually experience it. Second, as *philia* tends to occur between individuals of the same gender, there are fears that *philia* has homosexual connotations."

Tolkien, still standing, plucked his pipe from his mouth and gestured toward Jack. "Rubbish! You know as well as I do that *erōs*—erotic love—and *philia* certainly have a number of differences."

"Naturally," replied Jack. "But there are times when they mix, as they should within marriage, for instance. At any rate, as I said, many people do not experience true *philia*."

"Why do you think that is the case?" said Warren.

Williams interjected, "I think you know as well as I, Warren. Our culture tends to be fragmented and fast paced. In an environment where the focus is on the self and its pleasures, on the pursuit of material gain and success in life, as they say, there is little room for the building of true friendship. Genuine *philia* takes time, something that is unfortunately lacking in such a fragmented culture, or shoved aside rather." Williams smiled faintly at me, then began writing in his notebook again.

"But even *philia* has its dangers," said Tolkien.

"Dangers? Naturally there are dangers even in *philia*," said Jack.

"The inner ring," whispered Williams.

"What?" said Tolkien. "Did you say something about a ring?"

"Not that ring! How he does go on about rings," muttered Warren under his breath.

"The inner ring," repeated Williams, just as softly as before, but subtly emphasizing the phrase.

"Yes! The inner ring is a danger," said Jack.

"What is 'the inner ring'?" I asked.

"Well, for one, it's the title of an essay Jack wrote," said Tolkien, "as well as a concept he capably demonstrated in *That Hideous Strength*."

"The inner ring refers to an unhealthy cliquishness," said Jack, "wherein one is constantly trying to be a member of an elite group. There are no real friendships within the inner ring, but the seeker of such groups desires power and a certain elevated state of self worth. Such groups can lead to pride. The inner ring syndrome can come about via *philia* if members of such a group begin to see themselves as above or better than those not in the group. The Inklings, for instance, could have turned into an inner ring even though its basis was *philia*."

"And what of *storgē, erōs* and *agapē?*" I asked, uncertain about whether or not I had pronounced the Greek words correctly.

"*Storgē* is more of affection than love," said Williams. "That does not mean it is not one of the loves, but it is of a different sort. One might feel *storgē* for a pet, for instance, as well as for a person."

"Yes," said Jack, "making *storgē*—affection—distinct from *erōs*, meaning erotic love, which is found between lovers. Charles has spent quite a bit of effort developing this concept in relation to romantic love."

"I've made some real progress too," remarked Williams.

"And *agapē?*" I asked.

"Charity," said Warren.

"Right," added Tolkien, "but again we find ourselves in a position wherein our words fail us—or at least fall short of truly capturing the meaning behind the word. 'Divine love' captures a little bit more of what *agapē* is about."

"Indeed," said Jack, "divine love is supreme—a great gift to be cherished. Only God can provide real meaning to us and our lives, and he does it largely through the gift of his divine love. Friendship of the *philia* kind is one thing—we stand side by side and look upon what we appreciate as friends—what we admire in common. Lovers stand face to face. But with *agapē* we encounter the divine gift—God's love."

"You believe that *agapē* holds the loves together?" I asked.

"Yes. Without charity the other loves become weak, unable to truly function as they should. True friendship, then, is still of great value. I think most of the real happiness in this often miserable world comes from it."

"That seems a reasonable conclusion," I said.

"Speaking of reason, Tom," said Jack, "you seem a reasonable fellow. And yet I see a gaping flaw in your reason for trusting in reason."

"How so?" I asked, cautious of Jack's proven debating skills.

"Ah, the reason for reason," Warnie said, smiling and rapping his knuckles on the table. "Do you still think the argument works? I mean, after Anscombe?"

"Who's Anscombe?" I asked.

"I must have missed that too," said Williams.

"Oh, do let's give Jack a chance to make the argument and not go on about Elizabeth," said Tolkien. "Anscombe wasn't trying to disprove Christianity, you know. She honored the Mother Church, just like me."

"Quite right, Tollers," replied Jack. "Well, getting back to my comment, Tom, you seem a reasonable fellow—that is to say, you appear to take great stock in the power of reason to arrive at viable conclusions. Am I right in saying that?"

"Yes, of course," I said. "Reason, properly applied, can tell us a great deal. Naturally I take issue with religious types thinking they can apply reason to fairy tales and myths like the dying and rising god and such, but in general, yes, it is true that I find reason indispensable when it comes to ferreting out truth and error."

"As you should, young man," said Warnie.

"And yet," continued Jack, "am I right in saying that you believe human beings are the products of time and chance—a cosmic accident, if you will, a random mishap of undirected evolution?"

"I don't know that I'd put it quite like that, but as for humans being the product of chance, that is the obvious option for an atheist." I remembered Jack saying something along these lines to Kirkpatrick earlier.

"What, then, is your basis for explaining human reason?" Jack said, slowing his pace a bit, with deliberate precision. "If human beings are products of chance, then our reasoning abilities are also products of chance. Why, then, should we trust reason? Who's to say that our randomly produced reason can in any way grasp truth? On the basis of naturalism, there is no reason to trust reason."

"Go on," I said.

"Better to quote Professor Haldane, I think," suggested Tolkien.

"Good idea, Tollers," said Jack. "Haldane—no friend of Christianity, mind you—said, 'If my mental processes are determined wholly by the motions of atoms in my brain, I have no reason to suppose that my beliefs are true . . . and hence I have no reason for supposing my brain to be composed of atoms.'"

My mind began sifting through the many possible answers to Jack's argument. On the one hand, he seemed to make a good point. Why is it that we trust reason even though it is, from my atheistic point of view, a random product of "undirected evolution," as Jack put it? On the other hand, the argument seemed to me almost a trick, like a clever philosopher pulling out the ontological argument—"God must exist because he is the greatest conceivable being" and all that nonsense. I would have to proceed carefully in order to avoid Jack's trap. I'd also have to be convincing in my resolve.

"Well, I think it is clear that human reasoning is capable of grasping truth to a certain extent," I said. "We can, for instance, successfully conduct scientific experiments, perform mathematical calculations, arrive at viable conclusions and such."

"But on the basis of naturalism, how is it that we can trust our reasoning abilities?"

"I don't know that I grasp your point, Jack. After all, here we are reasoning. Are you saying we can't reason?"

"No, that's not my point at all. I agree that we can reason and that we are reasoning right now. My objection is to the claim that our reasoning is valid—perhaps veridical is a better term—on the basis of naturalism."

"I think," interjected Tolkien, "that Jack is concerned that if human beings are really the products of mere chance—undirected evolution—rather than directed intelligence, there seems to be little reason to trust reason—or, at any rate, a sound explanation for reason eludes us."

"Hear, hear!" boomed Warnie.

Tolkien cleared his throat and said, "But what of Anscombe? She did not think your argument succeeded."

"Not in its original form, no," said Jack. "But after my revision she complimented the improvements made."

Seeing my chance to gain some time to think, as well as apparently relevant information, I asked, "Who is Anscombe?"

"G. E. M. Anscombe or, if you prefer, Elizabeth Anscombe," said Warren. "She was a philosopher and Roman Catholic—"

"What of it?" Tolkien said, laughing.

"Yes, quite," said Warren. "Elizabeth was a philosopher and a Christian. One evening at a meeting of the Oxford Socratic Club, she got into a debate with Jack about a chapter in his book *Miracles.* This chapter argued along similar lines to what you heard Jack present just now—that on the grounds of naturalism there is no reason to trust reason. Well, Anscombe disagreed and found Jack's argument lacking."

"And some claimed Jack was so crushed by her philosophical blows," said Tolkien, "that Jack despaired, never to write works of apologetics again—the poor thing." Tolkien laughed.

"Rubbish!" said Jack with a smile. "I admit Elizabeth made some good points, which is why I revised that chapter of *Miracles* for a later printing. Nevertheless, I still believe the argument has merits. At any rate, it is not Elizabeth I am having a discussion with now, is it? Besides, as you noted, Warren, she was a believer. Her criticisms came as a philosopher, and in the end they sharpened rather than shattered my argument."

We talked a bit longer, most of it banter between the Inklings. After awhile, Jack stood and we said our goodbyes, leaving the parlor and moving to the main entrance of the pub. Jack asked Warren to follow.

"Warnie, would you be so kind as to return these overalls and boots to Paxford?"

"Of course."

"But I'm still wearing them, Jack!" I protested.

"Well, take them off, then. You won't be needing them where we'll be going next."

"Are you sure?"

"Yes, I'm sure. Of all the places we've been, believe me when I say that you'll fit right in at our next stop—at least when it comes to your attire."

I hesitated, but carefully removed the overalls and handed them over to Warren, who carried them back into the parlor.

"Now what?" I asked, feeling particularly out of place standing in a pub wearing nothing but my hospital gown—my feet bare once again.

Jack walked behind the bar and began to serve me a drink. *Finally,* I thought, *a cold beer right from the tap of an English pub!*

"Take a drink," said Jack as he handed me the mug. "It's water, by the way."

"Water? Why not something stronger?" I asked.

"I don't think your doctor would approve, Tom. Didn't alcohol play a part in your current condition?"

"Yes, but . . . Well, drinking a glass of water is a bit more Lewis Carroll than C. S. Lewis, isn't it?"

I began to drink the refreshing water, finishing it in one swig. As I prepared to put the mug on the bar, I realized there was no mug or bar to be seen. Where had Jack taken me now?

❦ 9 ❧

Mrs. Lewis and
the Meaning of Grief

In which we meet the delightful Mrs. Lewis, discuss love, marriage and "chronological snobbery," and grapple with grief.

We were no longer in the Eagle and Child. Instead, I found myself standing in what appeared to be a hallway in a hospital. Momentarily disoriented, thinking that we had returned to my room, I looked around more carefully and noticed that it was not a familiar place.

"Jack, where are we now?"

"Wingfield-Morris Orthopaedic Hospital. I was married here. Well, the second time, at any rate."

"The second time?"

"I don't mean to say I was married to different women. I married my wife, Joy, in a civil ceremony so she could remain in England in 1956. It wasn't until 1957 that we were married here in this hospital in a religious ceremony—what we both considered a real marriage before God. Follow me."

We walked a short while down the hall. Jack was right about my fitting in. Although my gown was not exactly like those of other patients, it was similar enough for people not to take any particular notice of me. Of course, I could never be quite sure whether others could see me or not until we interacted with someone.

I followed Jack into a large room with several beds in it. We approached one bed in particular. Sitting in a chair next to it was a young man—a priest, by the way he was dressed, presumably Anglican given Jack's denominational orientation.

The woman in the bed did not look well. She was, Jack later explained, in her early forties when they were married in the hospital, but she looked to be ten years or more her age. Her head was propped on several pillows, her dark hair showing clearly against the bright sheets. She wore horn-rimmed glasses and an expression of amusement.

"Jack! I didn't expect you here so soon today," she said.

"Life is full of the unexpected, as you know, Joy," replied Jack, as he stooped to offer a hug to the woman.

The priest stood and greeted us. "Good to see you, Jack," he said, extending his hand.

"And you, Peter, it is always good to see you. This is a friend, Tom. And Tom, this is Reverend Peter Bide. Peter performed our wedding ceremony, here at Joy's bedside. We are both quite grateful for this service—and for his healing prayers."

"It was nothing, Jack."

"Oh, but it was. You see, Tom, no one else would perform the ceremony. Since Joy had been married before, there was some confusion about whether or not it was right to join us in matrimony. Peter here, disobeying the Bishop of Oxford—"

"Jack, please don't remind me," the priest said as he smiled. "I'm in enough trouble as it is. If you'll excuse me for a moment, I'll leave you two in the presence of the delightful Mrs. Lewis," said Reverend Bide politely, then left the room.

"Joy, this is—" began Lewis.

"Tom. I heard. Does Tom have a last name?"

"Clerk," I said.

"Thomas Clerk, or shall I say Doubting Scholar, allow me to introduce myself. I am Helen Joy Davidman Gresham Lewis, but, please, just call me Joy or things will get more complicated than they already are. I have more names than I'd like." She extended her hand and I shook it.

"Thank you, it's a pleasure to meet you."

"That remains to be seen, Mr. Clerk," she answered.

"Call me Tom."

"I can tell you're an American, anyway. And what brings you to travel here with Jack?" She had a distinct New York accent. Later I learned she was raised in the Bronx.

"That's sort of complicated. You see, I'm an atheist and—"

"Great! I used to be one too. Of course, I used to be a Communist as well. Now I'm a Jewish Christian or a Christian Jew—which is it, Jack?" By her playful tone, I don't think she expected an answer.

"You," said Jack, "are a delightful woman—and my wife."

Jack sat on the edge of the bed and motioned that I take Reverend Bide's chair. "I've been on something of a journey with Tom. We've been discussing all sorts of interesting things. I think what brings us here is you."

"I'm flattered."

"I think we are to discuss love, marriage and perhaps more."

"Well, why not?" replied Joy. "I'm not going anywhere."

I was not sure where to begin, nor that I wanted to. They both looked at me, expecting something. It was a strange situation. I knew little about Jack and Joy. I thought that Anthony Hopkins played Jack in the movie *Shadowlands*, but I could only recall the basic story.

"I'm afraid I don't know where to begin," I said. "How did the two of you meet?"

That seemed a safe opening question.

"Through letters," said Joy. "I had recently converted to Christianity, in part because of the influence of Jack's books, and decided to write to him."

"When Warnie first read me her letter, I knew that this one demanded my special attention. Her wit and intellect were clearly present. So I wrote back."

"We corresponded for a time," said Joy, "then I came to visit with my two boys—David and Douglas."

"We became friends, I suppose you could say."

"Of course we were friends!" said Joy.

"We fell in love, as they say," said Jack, "and eventually married."

"And do your views of marriage correspond to Christian ones—a bit old-fashioned, perhaps?" I asked, looking at Jack. I really wanted to say "antiquated" or "prudish," but with Mrs. Lewis in the room, that approach didn't seem proper.

Jack looked slightly puzzled, then said, "Chronological snobbery."

"What?"

"Oh," said Joy, "that's just Jack's way of picking on arguments or statements that seem to have at their foundation the idea that anything old is not worth considering intellectually, while new ideas are favored."

"Yes," said Jack. "Your comment, Tom, about views of Christian marriage being 'old-fashioned' is a form of chronological snobbery. The real issue is whether or not the Christian position on marriage is true. Before we move further in our discussion of this topic, however, you will need to explain what you mean by 'old-fashioned.'"

"I mean to say that Christianity's teachings on marriage are, in my view, no longer in step with the times. Its views about monogamy, divorce and so forth seem to me the remains of a Puritan past. Civilization, for the most part, has moved beyond such notions as chastity. Sexual liberation, to be blunt, makes more sense than the sexual suppression of Christianity."

"Jack, I can see you've had your hands full!" said Joy as she laughed. "Tom has kept you thinking, I'll bet." She gently squeezed his hand. "You look exhausted, though. Are you all right?"

"Yes, I'll manage," answered Jack.

"What amuses me, Tom," Joy said, "is the fact that when Jack gave his radio talks on Christian marriage he wasn't even married!" She laughed again.

"And I admitted as much," replied Jack. "My arguments, however, do not depend on whether or not one is married, but how one views the Bible and what it teaches about marriage. My views of marriage, in my assessment, correspond to what God has revealed. But there is one misconception you stated that I need to correct right off, Tom."

"What is that?"

"You made the distinction between 'sexual liberation' on the one hand and 'sexual suppression' on the other, did you not?"

"Yes. Christianity suppresses natural sexual impulses and behaviors, causing, for many, psychological damage."

"And I take it," said Joy, "that sexual liberation has no side effects whatsoever?" Her tone communicated a hint of sarcasm.

"Tom," said Jack, "you are assuming that Christianity is a religion that looks down on sexual behavior. That is not really the case. Properly interpreted, Christianity believes in sexual behavior and the joys of the physical body. God is not against physical pleasure for his creatures. He invented the material world and, unlike Gnostics who viewed matter as bad and spirit as good, God likes matter. After all, he invented it. The point of contention regarding Christianity and marriage, for most, involves the fact that biblically speaking, these sexual pleasures are to be reserved for marriage—one man and one woman, mated for life. For the Christian there are only two options, really—either total abstinence or marriage."

"And there is your old-fashioned view again," I said.

"Careful, Tom," commented Joy, wagging a finger. "You'll end up being called a chronological snob again."

"It's just that your position doesn't make sense, Jack," I said. "Human beings are evolved animals. There are no moral standards holding us to Christian views of sexual morality or marriage. I grant that for the proper functioning of society we must have some rules on the matter, but these are really merely social contracts to help society function better."

"Congratulations, Tom," said Jack. "You've touched upon one of the key differences of our views. You, being an atheist, see human beings as nothing more than—how did you put it?—'evolved animals.' Christians, however, see human beings as specially created, in the image of God, bound to function at our best when we function within the parameters established by our Creator. Christianity teaches that marriage is for life, not to ruin our joys or pleasures, but in order to enhance them within God's boundaries. Sexual union is meant for marriage. The Bible teaches that a husband and wife become 'one flesh'—we become one organism, really, joined physically and spiritually."

"But what about divorce, Jack?" said Joy. "Tom asked about that, too, you know. After all, I was divorced."

"Yes, I grant that divorce is a complication," said Jack. "But at its core, despite denominational disagreements on the specifics of divorce and whether it should be permitted or not depending on circumstances and such, all Christian churches throughout the ages have agreed that divorce is a very serious matter. Ideally, it should not happen. Marriage is not viewed as merely a simple contract that can be broken at any time. Marriage is meant for life, and the separation of the 'one flesh' is serious indeed. It is like a surgical procedure—the cutting of one organism into two."

This last comment certainly hit me hard. After all, I'd been married for five years prior to my divorce. Had I really taken part in cutting an organism in two? At times it had felt like that, but I didn't take it literally and I don't think Jack did either. I surmised that he meant, within Christian marriage, two people really do become so close as to be like one organism.

We spent more time talking with Joy. She laughed often, as did Jack. After a time we left her to rest and made our way back down the hallway we had first gone through when we arrived. Jack opened a door, and I expected to see a parking lot. Instead, I found myself somewhere quite different.

"I don't know this place. Where are we?"

Surprisingly, it was Jack who asked the question this time. Unfortunately, I knew all too well where we were.

"No, this can't be," I said softly. "What do you think you're doing?" I said louder, glaring at Jack.

"Me?"

"Yes, you! Is this some kind of attempt to play on my emotions or what?"

"I assure you, Tom, that I don't know where we are. But after all you've seen, I think you know that we can be just about anywhere," said Jack calmly.

"No! It's all in my head—a hallucination, my body breaking down . . . we can't be here."

"Where is here?" Jack looked around the room, puzzled.

"My home," I stammered, "but years ago, when I was married."

"But this is a child's room," said Jack.

I looked around. Yes, it was a child's room. I saw the familiar bed, the toys, the clothes, and began to weep.

"Tom, what is it?"

I finally managed to speak. "Jack, this was my daughter's room."

"Was?" he asked softly.

"Sophie died when she was just a little girl. She was only six. How could your loving God allow that?"

I started out composed, but became angry, not so much at Jack, but at the God I didn't believe in. Jack looked at me not with anger, but with grief. I saw a tear on his cheek, then another.

"I'm so sorry, Tom."

"After she died, I kept her room just like this—like it was the day she died. My wife—she couldn't take it. A year later we divorced. My life has been something of a mess ever since."

"I see. I think we've been here long enough, don't you?"

"Yes, I think so."

"Is there a wardrobe?" asked Jack, looking around the room.

"No, I'm afraid not."

"What is that?"

"The closet."

"Let's try that then."

Jack opened the closet door. As he entered and I followed I noticed we were no longer in my daughter's room. Instead I saw a sunny day—green grass, trees and a path that led to a long structure. Jack began following the path to the building. We entered the brick archway and continued the walk in silence. I realized now that we were in a cemetery—near a crematorium, I think. All along the brick walls I saw plaques—memorials to the dead, but really for the benefit of the living. A short time later Jack stopped in front of a wall and stared at it in silence.

Curious, I too looked at the plaques and read various epitaphs. Then my eyes wandered to a larger, more prominent plaque and I shuddered.

"I wrote it," said Jack softly.

I stepped closer and read the epitaph to myself . . .

Remember

HELEN JOY
DAVIDMAN
D. July 1960
Loved wife of
C. S. LEWIS

Here the whole world (stars, water, air,
And field, and forest, as they were
Reflected in a single mind)
Like cast off clothes was left behind
In ashes, yet with hope that she,
Re-born from holy poverty,
In lenten lands, hereafter may
Resume them on her Easter Day.

I turned away. It couldn't be. I had just been at the hospital with this woman—had just talked and joked with her.

Jack, noticing my movement, finally broke our silence with a choked voice. "It was hard, you know . . . losing her. I loved her more deeply than I had ever loved anyone. I can't say that I know exactly what you went through when your daughter died, Tom, but I can say that I know grief beyond words."

Jack did not look well. He must have interpreted my concern.

"I can see from your expression," said Jack, tears now flowing, "that I can no longer conceal my condition."

"What condition?" I asked.

"You see, Tom, the longer I am with you, the more I revert to my mortal condition—the more I once again feel the pains of life, both physical and emotional." He pulled a handkerchief from his pocket and began to wipe his eyes.

"We spoke earlier, in the trenches, of the problem of evil," said Jack, his voice shaking slightly, but growing stronger now. "If you will recall, I explained that the problem of evil was best approached in stages or portions. We addressed the intellectual aspect. Certainly, we were in the trenches, but our experience was not the same as that of the soldiers. And now we come to the emotional aspect of the problem of evil, when suffering or grief or hardships—whatever one wishes to call the tribulations of life—hit us on a personal level."

"Go on," I said.

"You, Tom, lost a daughter. That is something I will not pretend to understand, but to say I know nothing of grief is far from the truth. I lost my beloved Joy, and I make no attempts to hide the pain I felt, nor my anger directed toward God. I recorded my thoughts in my book *A Grief Observed.* I called it 'a grief' because, though there are certainly similarities, I cannot presume to know what grief is like for anyone but myself."

"You had experienced grief before?"

"Oh, yes," replied Jack. "Every now and then a myth is raised about me—the myth that until the death of my wife I had not really experienced grief. The truth of the matter is that I had experienced grief far more often than I would have liked. My mother, as you know, died of cancer when I was a child. My father, many years later, also succumbed to the disease. My close friend, Charles Williams, died quite unexpectedly. But,

I admit, the death of Joy was different. We had merely a few short years together as man and wife, but those years were, for both of us, very full."

"You said you were angry with God. Did you consider renouncing your beliefs?"

"I'm not sure I would phrase it that way, but yes, I had my say, driven by grief and emotion. I tried to twist God into something he is not. I began to suspect, if briefly, that perhaps God exists but he is not all-loving. Maybe he is a cosmic sadist—a torturer or vivisectionist rather than a surgeon or caregiver."

"But you abandoned that line of reasoning?"

"In the end, I had to. I knew enough about God to know that was not really the case. Absolute moral law demands that God exist. The reality of evil cannot be called evil without a standard of righteousness—a standard God provides. The question then becomes, is God who the Bible claims he is or not, or is evil what we really think it is or not? Now we are back to the intellectual problem of evil. You see, our intellect and emotion are intertwined. That does not make the grief any less, but we cannot simply go on just feeling. There must also be time to think."

"What is your solution, then, to the emotional problem of evil?"

He looked at me, his gentle eyes still gleaming with his tears, "Tom, I don't know that I have a solution to this aspect of the problem that will suit everyone. To struggle with grief is something very personal, experienced in different ways by different people. To presume to have a suitable answer is something I am not foolish enough to say. I don't claim to know whether there is a purpose for every evil in this world. Indeed, that is something none of us, Christian or atheist, may ever know for certain. But I do know that God is not a God of hate, but of love. Grief is real, but its reality does not disprove God's existence."

"Come," said Jack, "let us move on."

❧ 10 ❧

Devil in the Gray Town

Wherein I am separated from Jack, wander deeper into a gray town, meet a dragon and have a surreal conversation with a devil.

We walked in silence for a short while. The weather had changed. Everything looked gray and uninviting; it began to rain. Jack made his way to a bus stop, where a magnificent double-decker bus loomed before us. In contrast to its dingy surroundings, the bus seemed to shine brilliantly golden. It looked like the bus I almost ran into when we were riding the Daudel.

The last of the passengers in the line boarded the bus, and Jack also got on. I followed. The driver, a carefree looking man with dark hair and beard, one hand on the wheel, seemed to know Jack and waved him by. "Follow Jack to the upper level, if you please," he said as I approached.

Jack had told me that the more time he spent with me, the more time he spent recalling his life, the more he would weaken and become almost mortal again. As I approached his seat at the back of the bus, I noticed he looked tired. Our trip to Joy's grave had taken its toll on him, as the trip to my daughter's room had taken its toll on me. He smiled weakly and motioned to the seat next to him.

"Where are we going now?" I asked as I sat down.

"This bus will take us to the world of the imagination—my world of imagination, to be more precise. In my book *The Great Divorce*, a bus took passengers from hell to heaven, so it seemed a fitting way for us to get to the topic of imagination."

I was irritated. "Really, Jack, you don't mean to say you really believe in hell? I live in modern times. Fire and brimstone have no effect on me, other than to demonstrate another relic of Christianity. You don't really believe your loving God would torture people forever in hell, do you? And what of Joy? Your God took her from you after only a few short years. And my daughter? What of her?"

Jack started to reply, but I'd had enough. I stood up.

"Where are you going, Tom?"

"I'm leaving!"

"Please stay. I don't know that I can help you if you willingly leave. Besides, you might not like what you find on your own."

But my anger moved me to ignore his warning. I quickly turned away. As I left the bus, I could hear the bearded driver calling to me, "Be careful—this is not the best place to go exploring."

I wandered through the gray and lifeless town for what seemed like hours. I thought it would get dark, but this place always seemed to hover at twilight. Finally, I spotted a structure different from the others. It was tall and looked like an office building. A broken lamp post near the entrance flickered yellow light on and off. As I approached, I noticed a crooked sign hanging over the doorway: "All hope abandon ye who enter here . . ." Still sulking over my outburst with Jack, I shrugged and entered the building.

I was in what appeared to be the lobby. A large, curved concrete counter—unattended—dominated the room. Papers were strewn about on the floor as well as the counter. Before I had time to examine the room more carefully, a shrill voice spoke from the speaker system overhead.

"Clerk, Thomas, follow the black line. Patient Clerk, Thomas, follow the black line."

I looked around and noticed a black line on the floor. It went as far as the counter, then stopped. I followed it, and as I neared the counter, the dark line extended itself several more feet, around the counter. In this manner, after wandering through this dingy building for some ten minutes, I arrived at an office door. The nameplate read, "Flubgose, Devil First Class." I stared at the closed door for a moment, then it creaked open.

Tentatively, I peeked inside. A concrete desk littered with paperwork was on one side of the room. Seated behind it, reclining in a swivel chair, was what I can only describe as a cartoonish-looking devil. I estimated it was between four and five feet tall. Its dark red leathery skin contrasted sharply with the drab grays of the concrete desk and largely unadorned walls. I did notice a framed photograph, askew, on one wall. On it was a photograph of what appeared to be the same devil as the one in the chair before me, though in the portrait he wore a black bowtie and a fiendish grin. At the bottom of the portrait were the words, "Tempter of the Month."

The devil looked up at me and smiled. As he leaned back in his chair, I thought I caught a glimpse of a long tail.

"I am Flubgose." He beamed, speaking in a quick staccato voice (bureaucratic, I thought), then remarked nonchalantly, "Devil First Class. You are Clerk. And you have a dragon on your head."

"Excuse me?"

"A dragon—you have one on your head. Sit down." He began to chew on a cigar, a subtle smirk on his face.

Unsure of how to respond, but well aware of my supposed entry into the world of imagination, I carefully felt the top of my head with both hands as I sat in a chair in front of the desk. There did not appear to be anything on my head.

"I don't feel anything," I said.

Flubgose opened a desk drawer and removed a mirror with an ornately carved handle. On it I recognized the masks of drama—a sad face (tragedy) and a happy one (comedy).

"Look at this." He placed the mirror on his desk and, with a sudden, precise and unexpected movement, shoved it over to me. I grabbed it just in time to rescue it from sliding onto the floor.

"Well, my dear Mr. Clerk, don't you want to see your dragon?" The devilish smirk had turned into a nasty grin.

Slowly I lifted the mirror and held it up so that I could see the top of my head.

"Good God!" I gasped, dropping the mirror.

"Now, now, there's no need to curse Our Prince Below with that kind of talk, is there, Mr. Clerk?" I don't think it would have been possible for Flubgose to smile more broadly.

I suddenly wondered why I did not hear the crash of the mirror I had dropped. I looked around for some semblance of reality, but saw instead that the mirror was hovering near me. I moved my hands around it, looking for string or wire—anything to explain the floating mirror.

"Tell me what you saw," said Flubgose.

"A black dragon, about the size of a large rat. At least, that's what I think I saw."

"That's Nigel."

"What?"

"Nigel. I looked it up in your case file." He grabbed a black folder from his cluttered desk and began flipping through it. "Nigel is the dragon assigned to your mind. He helps maneuver your thoughts in a downward direction. Now and then he puts thoughts into your mind, but mostly he just keeps them out." Flubgose uttered these absurdities as easily as if he were ordering a cup of tea.

"The dragon has a name?" I asked, incredulous.

"Of course he does. Nigel, speak." Flubgose broke eye contact and instead looked to the top of my head. I felt with both my hands, but could find no dragon.

"You can't find him that way, fool. That's why I gave you the mirror. Take it and look again." I hesitated. "Do it!" He paused. "You know you want to." Then he laughed.

I took the mirror and, hands slightly shaking, held it up again. There he was—a small black dragon, looking rather vicious, but also somewhat weary. He seemed to sigh, and as he did, puffs of smoke came out of his nostrils. He walked around my head in circles a few times, like a dog getting ready to nap, lay down and folded his bat-like wings against his body.

"Nigel!" yelled Flubgose. "Get up and speak." It was not a request.

"Oh, what's the point?" The dragon spoke in a high, raspy voice. "I'm tired. This bloke 'as been thinkin' too much lately—makes more work for me, see? How 'bout you jus' lemme' take a li'l ol' nap, Mr. Flubgose? I've been workin' on this fellow a long time now and I figures I deserves a li'l break while you two chat."

"Fine, Nigel. You've made your point for my purposes. But your behavior will be noted in my report." The devil made a notation in the black folder then set it on the desk.

I placed the mirror face down on the desk. This was too much. What was Flubgose trying to do? If his intention was to make me insane, he was off to a good start.

"You don't think all your thoughts are your own, do you?" said the devil. "Nigel helps you see things our way, Mr. Clerk. Oh, don't get the wrong idea. Nigel spends most of his time keeping ideas out of your head, as I said, but sometimes he makes an effort to put ideas in your head or divert your train of thought. Up until recently he's been doing a fine job of it as far as I can tell from your case file." He tapped the black folder with his fingers.

The devil leaned back in his chair, put his cloven-hoofed feet on his desk and perused the contents of the black file folder. I could just make out the following words printed on the outside of it: "Patient: Clerk, Thomas. Status: Undetermined." At this moment I heard the door slam closed behind me. I turned my head and saw the locks closing.

"Listen here," I said, trying to muster some forcefulness, "I don't quite get your angle yet with all this Nigel the dragon nonsense, but I have rights. I demand you let me leave this place at once!"

"You—rights—demand—leave!" Flubgose sat up and scowled, placing the folder on his desk and bringing his hands together, interlocking his fingers, elbows on his desk. "My dear Mr. Clerk, you brought yourself here, so why do you want to leave so soon?"

"What do you mean, I brought myself here?"

"It's true. You had a little spat with that idiot Jack on the bus, stomped off in your anger, and here you are."

"He's not an idiot!" I didn't expect to say that, but it came out.

"Oh, so he's your best friend now, is he? That's not what your behavior on the bus demonstrated, was it?"

Jack was probably still on the bus. He said he might not be able to help me if I left him, but right now I needed his help. After all, this was supposedly Jack's imaginary world.

My reaction to the devil's words surprised me. I did not intend to defend Jack, but my visit to this strange place and the devil's harsh words aimed at Jack bothered me. I didn't see eye to eye with Jack on many fronts—the existence of God, the solution to the problem of evil, the claims of Christ—but this devil, Flubgose, made me realize that I considered Jack a friend. He had not treated me as inferior or belittled my skepticism. Quite the contrary, Jack had shown himself to be a gentle man, respectful of my beliefs but firm in his convictions.

I stood up. "You made a mistake in attacking Jack. I may not agree with him or his beliefs about Jesus"—Flubgose cringed at the name—"but, unlike you, he's earned my respect and my friendship. I'm leaving now." I made my way to the door.

"Sit down! You can't leave!" Flubgose yelled.

"Watch me." I tried to turn the locks, but couldn't. I didn't know what else to do, but call for help from Jack. "Jack! Help! It's Tom!"

"Sit down!" yelled Flubgose again. "Stop that yelling! Nigel, stop him!"

He stood up now, looking irritated and, I thought, slightly fearful, but stayed behind the desk. The door opened. I saw the drab hallway with the black line and debris scattered about, but it was bent somehow—swirling as though it were being reluctantly flushed down a drain. I heard faint footsteps approaching then saw Jack moving toward me. As he arrived at the doorway he extended his right hand.

"You must reach out and take my hand, Tom," said Jack calmly.

"Sit down, Clerk! You can't leave! I am Flubgose—Devil First Class and Tempter of the Month!" cried the creature behind me, pounding his fists on his desk. "You!" He pointed at Jack. "You must leave at once!"

"I am a servant of the Most High," answered Jack, "bought with the blood of the Lamb"—Flubgose cringed again—"and will leave when I please."

I took Jack's hand, and he pulled me through the doorway. I looked back into the office and saw Flubgose, jaw open. Then his entire office disappeared in a whirlpool of colors and sounds. The next moment we were back at the bus stop, the golden double-decker bus parked before us, glistening despite the gray world around it.

"Thank you, Jack. And," I said, "I'm sorry for my outburst."

"Don't let it trouble you," said Jack, graciously. "We all have our outbursts now and then."

"But I should have treated you better. You've—you've been so kind. I don't agree with your beliefs, but I'd be honored to call you a friend."

"Likewise. Now, let us continue our journey. We're getting very near the end."

We stepped on the bus, took our seats and resumed our journey as the bus rolled slowly forward before unexpectedly lifting off the ground with all the grace and power of an eagle.

Narnia and the
World of Imagination

Of assorted events mainly centered on the role of imagination, the Narnia chronicles, and Jack's insights on faith, fantasy and philosophy.

The bus landed gently. As the door opened, we exited. Unlike the dreariness of the gray town, bright daylight now surrounded us. Storybook clouds filled the vivid blue sky—white and cotton-like. Jack pointed to a hill. I looked up and saw large golden gates at the top.

"I thought the gates were pearly," I said, smirking.

"That's not where we are. Come, let's ascend."

As we reached the top of the hill, an extraordinary and amusing sight greeted me. I saw a mouse about two feet tall, with strikingly dark fur, wearing a thin gold circlet on its head. The circlet held a large crimson feather. As we approached, the diminutive creature, rapier at his side, first bowed, then spoke.

"Welcome, Sir Jack!" it squeaked. I almost laughed, but a stern look from Jack warned me against such behavior.

"It is a joy to see you again," said Jack, smiling. "May I—"

"Very well, if you must," answered the creature. "But only once."

Jack reached down, picked up the animal and gave it a gentle hug before setting it down again.

"And this, Sir Jack, must be your squire?" The diminutive creature looked in my direction, his piercing black eyes showing no fear, but rather boldness with a hint of disdain. It lifted its right hand to its face and began to twirl a whisker.

"No, this is Tom. He is my guest."

"I see. Enter, then, the world of Sir Jack's imagination."

The mouse gave another low bow. He gestured to the golden gates, and as he did so they slowly opened. I noticed a plaque on one of the gates, which read, "Art thou for something rare, and profitable? Wouldest thou see a Truth within a Fable?"

Before I had time to ask Jack about the plaque, the gates were fully opened. I gasped at the sight before me. In the distance to my right I saw four children clothed in winter coats making their way through an area of snowy woods—an open wardrobe near them, much like the one I had stepped through earlier. The children stopped at a lamp post, apparently pausing to discuss something. Not too far from them I saw what looked like animals climbing out of the earth. Lower on the horizon a flying horse began its descent—two children riding upon it.

I turned to my left and saw colorful floating islands. A small red serpent, a seemingly gentle dragon (unlike Nigel), stretched its wings then curled up near a tree. I thought I caught a glimpse of a green-skinned woman dashing through the strange foliage. I looked up and saw a spherical spaceship of some kind, soaring against the backdrop of a starry sky.

In the distance loomed an enormous mountain; only it wasn't a mountain, but a giant. A woman on a horse approached it (or him), a determined look on her face. She held a gleaming sword in her hands.

The clanging of swords from another direction caught my attention. I looked and saw a veiled woman, fighting fiercely against a man. A crowd gathered round them. In another direction I saw an eerie castle. In the courtyard were countless statues of various mythological creatures—a centaur, a giant, dwarves, several animals.

Further away, upon a hill, I could barely make out a great golden lion gazing over all the scenes. Even though he was far away, his presence made me uncomfortable. He seemed to look everywhere. And yet, he also seemed to look right at me.

Startled, I saw a large brown bear bounding in our direction, much too close for my tastes. A man appeared to be chasing the beast.

"Jack! Let's get out of here," I implored. But Jack stood his ground. The bear reached us, stood up on its hind legs and began to lick Jack's face.

Jack beamed. He hugged the bear, which seemed to placate it somewhat, and it got down on all fours again. At this point the man chasing the bear arrived, yelling. "Mad bear, what have I told you about scaring visitors!"

The man, who carried a soap-covered scrub brush, spoke with what sounded like a thick Scottish accent, though Jack later said the man was from Ulster.

"Sorry, sirs," he said to us. "He always gets that way come bath time."

"No problem at all," said Jack.

"Mr.—?" said the Ulsterman.

"Lewis. Jack Lewis. Call me Jack."

"And who might you be?" said the man, looking at me.

"I'm Thomas Clerk."

"Escaped from a hospital, did you?" he asked.

"It's complicated," I replied.

"And might you know where we are?" inquired the man with the scrub brush.

"We are in a representation of the world of my imagination," said Jack calmly.

"And do you have any proof—any, that is, veridical evidence that this is the case?" The thought had occurred to me as well.

"Look around you," answered Jack, gesturing at the many scenes taking place around us.

The man gazed around, taking in the same incredible sights I first saw upon entering through the golden gates.

"Good point," he said. "But maybe we are just dreaming or hallucinating."

The bear went bounding off in another direction and the man went chasing after him.

"This is your imagination?"

"Yes," said Jack. "Well, some of it, at any rate."

As I prepared to make a comment to Jack, I noticed something shocking.

"Are you all right, Tom?"

"No, I'm not! Can't you see what's happened to me?"

I held up my hand and turned it before Jack's face. "I'm transparent."

In fact, I could look through my own hand and see Jack's puzzled face right through what once was flesh and bones. A disturbing thought occurred to me.

"Jack, am I . . ."

"Dead? No, not quite."

"What's happened to me then?"

His face lit up for a moment. "Yes, that must be it!"

"What?"

"We are in the world of my imagination, but in a broader sense we are in the world of imagination in general. The fact that you are transparent—translucent, really—leads me to conclude that your imagination, or rather your lack of imagination, is resulting in your present condition."

"I don't understand."

"Let me put it bluntly. You, Tom, lack imagination—at least a well-developed imagination. You are certainly a reasonable enough fellow, though I've noted several flaws in some of your ideas, but imagination, you know, is important, too. At any rate, my best guess based on available data is that you are translucent in this realm because your imagination requires some improving."

"I'm not sure I understand."

"Come, let's find a place to sit and talk."

After a brief walk, we stopped before a small stone table. Even though this area was surrounded by snow, for some reason I did not feel cold despite the fact that I wore only a hospital gown. Several statues were seated around the table—there were squirrels, a dwarf, a fox and others I could not identify. One little squirrel looked as though it were beating the table with a spoon. Laid out on the surface I saw a great stone feast, cold and obviously inedible. Jack sat down on a bench, as if we were in the most natural place in the world. Wondering if my transparent body would be able to sit, I moved carefully to a seat opposite Jack.

"Imagination is something I devoted much thought to during my earthly life," said Jack. "After I became an atheist, exalting logic and in general the abilities of human reasoning, I was puzzled by the fact that my imagination still held a great sway over me. Once again I confronted the draw of elusive desire. Intellect, you see, while certainly having its place, is incomplete without imagination."

"How so?"

"For me, at any rate, the draw of desire and longing for joy could not be touched through intellect alone. It was the world of imagination that provided glimpses of joy to me. After I became a Christian, I would say that my view of imagination grew—gradually, of course, but it grew nonetheless. For a time—"

A sound interrupted us. Three of the stone squirrels were transforming into living creatures, and one of them, a smaller one, squealed. Following their transformation the squirrels looked at us, then at the little stone squirrel with the spoon, then they ran off, hiding behind a nearby tree, occasionally popping out from behind it, as if spying on us.

"What happened?" I asked, turning to Jack.

"My presence must have awakened them," he answered.

"At any rate," he said, "as I was saying, for a time I still emphasized reason even in my works of fiction. This can be seen, I think, in my trilogy beginning with *Out of the Silent Planet.* Of course there are imaginative elements, but the main thrust of the series, particularly in the concluding volume *That Hideous Strength,* is on reason. I asked myself how I could show the outcome, in a modern fairy tale, of the thinking I discussed in *The Abolition of Man.* It was later, however, that I believe I truly began to reconcile reason and imagination—"

The dwarf, grunting, and the fox, yawning, now caught our attention. They, too, were transforming. Taking one look at us, the fox swiftly ran off. The dwarf paused a moment, as though considering whether or not to speak, then ran off in another direction. I looked at the remaining stone creatures, just three of them, waiting for something to happen.

"What are those two?" I asked Jack, pointing to a couple of goat-legged creatures with pointed ears and horns on their heads. "Are they—fauns?"

"Satyrs," Jack said. "Fauns are only half-goats and generally smaller, at least in my stories. But they do share some similarities. They are one of the nine classes of Narnian creat—"

"Thanks, Jack. I get the idea."

As we spoke, the two satyrs began their transformation. The first to transform looked startled, frightened even. "Goodness gracious me!" he exclaimed. He turned to the other satyr, who had just completed his transformation. "Run!" he whispered, and run they did—away from us. Hearing more squeals, I turned and looked in the direction of the tree where the three squirrels had run off moments ago. There they were, hiding behind the tree, peering at us again.

"What do they want?" I asked Jack.

"But there is one left," said Jack, looking at the little stone squirrel still seated at the table, clutching a tiny spoon. And as we looked, the tiny creature transformed into a living being with a loud high-pitched voice.

"He has, he has, he has!" squeaked the squirrel as it repeatedly beat the table with the spoon. "Father Christmas is here and Aslan is on the move!"

Then, for the first time, it noticed us. I heard more squeaks coming from nearby. At that instant the little squirrel dropped the spoon and ran to the tree, where the other three squirrels embraced the newcomer, then they all scampered up into the tree and out of sight.

"I think that will put an end to our interruptions," Jack said with a smile. "Now, what was I saying?"

"Something about reconciling reason and imagination, I think."

"Yes, quite right. I found that I could communicate the truths of Christianity through fantasy. I could discuss theology and philosophy without the usual barriers involved in reaching people who might otherwise be uninterested in such matters. I could, instead, do it without coming across as preachy. You could say I went from being metaphorically translucent about imagination—much like you are now—to being solid or at least becoming more solid."

"I don't know, Jack. For me reason seems superior to imagination. I'm not saying imagination doesn't have its place, but I don't really see much value in it beyond providing some entertainment."

"I think that is because in your day imagination, like a great many other concepts, has been twisted. Imagination can indeed be entertaining, but entertainment merely for the sake of entertainment is devoid of the potency of what imagination can truly accomplish in the hands of a master such as Dante or even Bunyan. When we entered this realm, do you remember the plaque on the gates?"

"Yes, I meant to ask you about it."

" 'Art thou for something rare, and profitable? Wouldest thou see a Truth within a Fable?' " Jack quoted. "That is John Bunyan, as quoted from the opening portion of *Pilgrim's Progress.* Bunyan, you see, uneducated and simple though some may see him, understood the power of imagination to communicate real truths, even within the setting of a fable or, in his case, an allegory. Therein lies one of the powers of imaginative literature—the power to do away with all the stained glass windows of religiosity, to sneak past such obstacles and slip in great truths about reality."

"And is that what you set out to do with your Narnian chronicles—to indoctrinate children into Christianity?"

"My goodness, you make it sound as though Narnia was designed from the ground up to convert unsuspecting children, snatching them from the clutches of atheist parents! That was hardly my method or my purpose. You're not the first to suspect that, however. People seemed to think that I did studies on children and what kinds of literature I could use to manipulate their little minds, then proceeded to inject all sorts of Christian theology into the books. That's not how it happened at all!"

"But there's no denying that your Narnia stories have a lot of Christian elements in them. I mean you have a character die and come back to life, Jack!"

"Tom, my stories have 'a lot of Christian elements in them,' as you put it because I am a Christian. A Buddhist writing stories would, I think, if he or she was serious about their religious beliefs, naturally include elements in the stories that tied into Buddhism. The same for a Hindu or Native American or atheist for that matter. We all have a worldview, whether we acknowledge it or not. And, yes, for writers it tends to come out in their writing."

"You have a point, but still—the Narnia stories seem a bit more overt to me."

"As a Christian—a devoted one and, I hope, a thinking one—my mind was always bubbling with ideas that grew naturally out of my sincere beliefs, not out of some story-producing machine designed to convert children."

"But what about the allegory of Narnia?" I objected.

"There is another mistake. People often think Narnia is allegory, when in reality it is not."

"But doesn't the lion stand for Christ and the witch for Satan?"

"No!" said Jack. "I'm afraid you are doing what many often do with the Bible—they read their own ideas into it rather than drawing out of it the true intended meaning. To me allegory is a very particular category of literature. Bunyan's *Pilgrim's Progress* is allegory, wherein certain ideas or principles are represented by characters or places and such. If you want allegory from me, the best I can give you is my book *The Pilgrim's Regress*. Narnia is another matter. Those stories have allegorical elements, but they are more supposals than allegory."

"What do you mean by 'supposals'?"

"I mean that when I began working on Narnia my starting point was not allegory, but supposal. Suppose there was a realm called Narnia. Suppose that it needed redemption. Suppose that it was populated by all kinds of fantasy creatures, such as talking animals. How might God redeem this world? Well, if we are dealing with mainly talking beasts, then God would become a beast, just as when he dealt with human beings he became a man in the person of Christ. If you give this 'supposal' approach some thought, especially in light of what true allegory really is, then you will see that what I did with Narnia is quite different from allegory."

"So Narnia is not allegory?" I remained unconvinced.

"It is not. As a literary scholar, you know, I did study the subject of allegory extensively. My first real success in my field was my book *The Allegory of Love*. I can assure you that Narnia is not true allegory. I will, however, grant that there are allegorical elements in Narnia."

"What is Narnia, then? Is it fable?"

"Now you've added another term—*fable*—into the mix. It is true that Aslan is sacrificed and that he comes back to life, but this does not make my story allegory."

"Isn't it true that one finds these elements—the dying god coming back to life—in many stories across various cultures?" I recalled our earlier conversation with Kirkpatrick about Frazer and *The Golden Bough*.

"Yes, quite so, and as I explained to you earlier, I believe those stories are merely hinting at God's 'true myth'—the reality of the death and resurrection of Christ. As far as Narnia 'indoctrinating' children, as you put it, that was certainly not my intent. Christian elements came into the stories naturally because of my beliefs. I did want, at the mythic or imaginative level, to allow children to glimpse certain truths of Christianity in story so that perhaps later in life they would recall these instances—such as the sacrifice of Aslan—and associate them with Christianity."

"So you did have an agenda?"

"I wouldn't call it an agenda, Tom. I believe the myths of various cultures do indeed contain elements or fragments of the great truths of

God's story, except in Christianity these fragmented truths coalesce into what I call the 'true myth' of Christianity—meaning that Christ really lived, really did all the things the New Testament claims, really died and rose from the dead for the sake of our redemption—should we choose to embrace it."

"Then Christianity is a myth, but you believe it's true?"

"You call Christianity a 'myth' and a 'fable' and in some respects you are right—there are mythic elements in it, but in Christianity they correspond to reality. You may put God in the dock—that is, on the witness stand—and hold a trial, but in the end his truths stand firm based on the evidences of reason, as well as history."

"Jack, you can't really expect me to believe all the nonsense in the Bible, can you? I mean, the blind receiving sight or a man walking on water?"

"It is only your presupposition that miracles cannot happen that keeps you from being open to their possibility," said Jack coolly.

"Have you read my Narnia books?" he asked.

Somewhat embarrassed, I replied, "Well, I've only read one of them— *The Lion, the Witch, and the Wardrobe*—but it's been many years."

"I suggest you read them all, then reconsider the question of allegory versus supposal, as well as your presupposition that the books are intended to 'indoctrinate.'"

Momentarily distracted by the sight of the large brown bear running in the distance, followed by the man with a scrub brush, I did not hear Jack's next question.

"What?" I asked, turning my attention back to our conversation.

"Do you consider yourself more a man of reason or imagination?"

"Well, reason, of course. What real purpose is there in imagination? Reason, however, I can get a handle on. The scientific method, rational inference—these are the things that I believe in."

Jack smiled.

"What is it?"

"You sound like me when I was an atheist."

"Well, then, I'd say you were probably on the right track back then."

"I certainly thought so. One problem I had, however, was that I enjoyed the world of imagination a great deal. As one of the few pleasures in my life, I treasured the realm of fantasy and imagination—the quiet step toward elf-land filled me with joy unspeakable. It was not, in fact, until many years later—even after my conversion to Christianity—that I felt as though I had reconciled reason and imagination."

"What's wrong with reason? Reason is worthy of reverence, isn't it?" I knew I had stumbled by choosing *reverence* to describe reason.

"I'm not quite sure what you mean by 'reverence' or what philosophical grounds you have as an atheist for even using terms such as 'reverence.' Reason is your 'god' of sorts, but at any rate I think you are missing the point. The reconciling of reason and imagination does not mean the abandonment of either. What I meant to indicate is that as my thinking in the area of reason and imagination progressed over time, I was able to produce works, such as Narnia, *Till We Have Faces* and *Letters to Malcolm*, that were highly imaginative, but still based on reason. I had, in effect, been freed from the struggle between my reason and my imagination and, in short, saw the two as playing important roles in my life."

"You value imagination, then, because—"

"The world of imaginative literature," continued Jack, "opens us to other ideas, other worlds—the great conversation of the ages, if you will. Are your own eyes enough for you, Tom? Would you not prefer to also see through the eyes and minds of others? To taste, to sample, to enjoy, to analyze, to ponder the worlds and ideas of a thousand men and women, rather than just your own?"

He did not expect me to answer these questions, but continued with an obvious passion for not only imagination, but clearly for the power of great literature.

"Don't limit yourself to only the world of reason—powerful and useful though it is. Reach out with your imagination in seeking to understand the world and all that is in it. See, you are becoming more solid already."

I looked at my hands again and could no longer see through them.

A long, loud roar caught our attention. I looked in the direction it came from and saw, on top of a large green hill, the lion I had seen when first passing through the gates. Not just any lion, but a very large one that seemed to glow.

"Is it dangerous?" I asked Jack. "I mean, is he tame—safe?"

"No." Jack smiled, pausing a moment. "But he's good."

I looked again and the lion had gone. Instead I saw a centaur galloping toward us. He was so large that I had to look up to see his eyes, which were deep and green.

"Welcome, Sons of Adam," said the centaur in a rich and resonant voice.

"Greetings," said Jack as he bowed before the great beast, motioning me to do the same.

"Long has it been since I have seen you, Sir Jack."

"And I you, Alethos."

"The Emperor's Son sends me as emissary. But who is this?" He looked at me.

"This is Thomas Clerk, a companion. Together we have journeyed far."

"Greetings, Thomas. I see that you are a troubled Son of Adam. Fear not. With Sir Jack as your guide, I am sure you are on your way to healing."

I nodded.

"Come," he said. We followed the great centaur back up the hill, where

I noticed three stakes of wood were set up like the frame of a doorway leading nowhere.

I felt a sudden urge to ask about the lion.

"May I . . . may I meet the lion?" I asked the centaur, hope stirring within me.

"He is ready to meet you . . ." My spirits rose, but after a pause Alethos continued, "But you are not ready to meet him. It is time for you to return to your own world, Thomas, but not yet to your own time. Look for the lion in the world of men, but he will not be a lion there."

I looked at the doorframe and in it I saw many wondrous things. First I saw Jack's childhood home, Little Lea—Jack and Warnie were once again digging a hole in the garden. Then I saw Jack's tutor, Kirkpatrick, at his home, still working the earth in his garden. This was followed by a scene showing Jack fighting in the trenches of World War I, but the image suddenly changed to Jack's comfortable rooms at Oxford, where he was tutoring students with his usual flair and passion. Then I saw the BBC studios, Jack sitting at a table in a recording studio. The Eagle and Child pub appeared next—Jack, Tolkien, Williams and Warnie were laughing heartily. The hospital where Jack married Joy appeared—Jack at Joy's bedside, holding her hand and reading to her—followed by the last scene, Jack's home, the Kilns. It looked peaceful, as it did when we visited it before.

"Farewell, Sons of Adam," said the great centaur. I had almost forgotten he was standing beside the doorway.

"Goodbye, Alethos," said Jack, bowing slightly.

"Bye," I added quietly, as we stepped through the frame and back to the Kilns.

Immortality, Hell and
the Great Story

In which we return to the Kilns, have some tea, discuss immortality, heaven and hell, and once again I am separated from Jack.

We stepped out and the wooden frame vanished. I placed a hand at my forehead, shielding my eyes from the sunlight.

"What now?" I said.

"It is time you entered my home, rather than just standing about," Jack replied. He made his way to the front door, opened it and entered.

It was smaller than I had expected. After all, in life Jack had served with Oxford and Cambridge and had written many successful books. I expected his home to be, well, more affluent looking, I suppose. It was apparent that material wealth and what it could purchase were of little interest to Jack. But nearly everywhere I looked I saw shelves, many of them floor to ceiling, lined with books—older, worn books as well as newer volumes. Many had escaped their captivity and were piled here and there on tables, desks and chairs. Something told me that Jack was no mere collector and had probably read most, if not all, of the books in his collection.

"Come, let us retire to the common room."

I followed Jack. Along the way I stopped and stared. Jack turned, sensing that I no longer followed.

"Is it—"

"Is it 'the one' from *The Lion, the Witch, and the Wardrobe?*" finished Jack. "Not particularly, but many have asked."

Before us stood a large, ornately carved wardrobe—the same one we had stepped through hours before in my hospital room.

"My grandfather carved it," said Jack proudly, as he reached out and touched it. "You wouldn't believe how many visitors want to open it and feel the back. Funny thing—most of them are adults. No worries, Tom. It is an ordinary wardrobe as far as I can tell. That is what made it the perfect choice for my story—the ordinary becomes extraordinary. But maybe you can try again later. Who knows? Perhaps there is some magic in it after all."

We made our way to what Jack called the common room. Against one windowed side I saw a chair in front of a cluttered desk. Next to it I saw a comfortable-looking upholstered chair. Beside it was a lamp. More bookshelves lined the walls. Jack sat in the upholstered chair and motioned me to a matching one I had not noticed.

"Jack?" I heard a voice approaching. "Jack, is that you?" Warren stood in the doorway, carrying a bundle. "Oh, it is you. Good to see you again, Tom. Here's today's post," he said, placing a rather large pile on the desk. "I'm getting some tea ready. Would you like some? And cakes too?"

"Yes, please, Warnie."

"Right, then. You might want to take a nap later, Jack. You look weary today." He turned and left.

"You have quite a bit of mail there," I observed.

"Yes. I don't know what I would do with it all if not for Warnie's assistance. It seemed to start—the increase in my post, that is—after my broadcast talks."

"And you answer them all?"

"Yes, except for the ones sent by madmen, signed by 'Jehovah' and such." He smiled.

"Surely you could find better things to do with your time."

"Could I?" He settled himself in his chair a bit, crossing his legs. "That depends on how one views people, I suppose."

"How do you mean?"

"Are people, even strangers, of any importance or are they not?"

"I merely meant to observe that they probably don't all expect an answer. You are busy and are only one person. They are fans, I suppose, eager to hear from a favorite author."

"Fans? I find the term amusing. Common courtesy demands that I reply. Besides, even strangers are made in the image of God—" *Here it comes,* I thought. "Hence, they are all worth my time. These are people, just like you and me, who are designed to live forever. We should all take the time for one another. Bustling about, ignoring people or treating them poorly is something none of us should do. Civility is required."

Warren returned with the tea. "Here you are," he said, setting a tray down on the desk.

"Thank you, Warnie. Will you be joining us?"

"No, I think I will have a bit of a read and a rest in my room." He turned and left. I would not see him again until later.

Jack picked up a teapot and poured himself a cup. "Would you like some?" he asked.

"Yes, please." He poured me a cup, and we sipped the delicious tea in silence for a few moments. And so it was.

"Now, where were we?"

"People?" I suggested.

"Yes, people. But what about people? Immortality."

"I don't believe in immortality. It is a childish sort of wishful thinking. A denial of the reality and finality of death."

"I expected as much. But then, here you are conversing with me?"

"You are a dream or a hallucination—my subconscious grappling with itself. Soon it will be over."

"As you wish. But the question of immortality is not a dream. It is a real issue."

"I've shared my position. After death we cease to exist. Everything that we are is no more. I admit it doesn't sound pleasant, but if God does not exist, if the universe is indeed the product of chance, then we are merely here for a short period and when we die that is the end of us."

"I agree that, given atheism, you have explained the most logical outcome. But what if Christianity is true?"

"Then I am wrong. But if atheism is true, then you are wrong. Or," I added, "we could both be wrong."

"Right, we are back to logic. The difference being that I believe the evidence is on my side. Humor me, if you would. Let us grant that immortality—that we will go on, in some form forever—is a reality."

"Fine, but just for the sake of argument."

"Well, then, if we are to live forever, then every human being is of utmost importance. Nations and even civilizations are of nothing in comparison for they will pass away. But even more important than our immortality is where we will spend eternity."

"You're not going to talk about hell, are you? What an old-fashioned, intolerable doctrine!"

"'Old-fashioned' takes us back to chronological snobbery, Tom. I'm afraid a discussion of hell is part of a discussion of immortality. Fortunately, we can also speak of more hopeful things such as heaven."

"I think I will find that discussion worse than one on hell. Heaven—playing harps, streets paved with gold. Do you mean, Jack, that you believe in such nonsense? Don't you see through it—don't you see that it is merely a ploy, the 'pie in the sky,' as they say?"

"I don't, and given your remarks I think the real question relates to truth—does the 'pie in the sky' exist or not? As to the imagery of harps and gold, you are referring to wonderful symbols meant to communicate—to hint to us—just a fragment of what awaits those who believe." He took a sip of his tea and reached for a cake. He took a bite and coughed.

"Are you all right, Jack?" He seemed to recover quickly, but he looked tired, somewhat flushed.

"I'm well enough, thank you. Now, Christianity teaches that every person is immortal. And ultimately everyone will face one of two eternal destinations—heaven or hell."

"And what of purgatory? I've heard that you believed in it. Isn't it a second chance for lost souls?"

"What always amazes me about interpretations of my view of purgatory is the fact that no one seems to stop to define the term or what it meant for me. In my view, purgatory is a place of cleansing for saved souls. It is not for those who reject God's truth. It is like having a tooth pulled—being cleansed after death. It is purgation, as in Dante—a purification for those who already believe."

"But what about *The Great Divorce?*" I objected. "You said in that book that people travel from hell to heaven."

"*The Great Divorce* is a theological fantasy—a dream," answered Jack. "Another supposal. I did not intend it to be read as a systematic theology. It is more a morality tale, more about the choices we as individuals make every day of our lives and how those choices influence our eternal destiny. Now, getting back to heaven and hell—"

"Wait a moment. Why only those options? Couldn't God have created a world where no one is lost?"

"Such a world, to put it in different terms, is one where everyone is saved. Universalism. Many would agree with you, but I think that gets us back to the question of free will. In the end, you see, there are some who will simply not believe. They want to be left alone and God grants them their wish."

"So they go to hell?"

"I don't revel in the doctrine of hell, Tom. In fact, if I could find a way to remove it from Christian teaching I would, but I'm afraid the doctrine is clear in the pages of Scripture and from the mouth of our Lord himself. Some will not repent. What is to be done with them? Leave them alone in a hell of their choosing."

"It still seems like there could be a better solution. Eternal suffering for temporary sins seems a bit much, don't you think? Why doesn't God just destroy these unbelievers?"

"You have made two points that require responses. First, is eternal suffering unfair given the fact that the punishment is for temporal sins—that is, sins committed during a finite lifetime? Second, is annihilation a viable alternative to hell? Let us address the first point."

"Go on."

"Your point, correct me if I am mistaken, is that hell appears unfair in light of the fact that it is, in the Christian view, said to be eternal. Yet those who are in hell have committed sins for only a set duration of earthly time. One is eternally damned for sin that is transitory. At a glance it does seem unfair, doesn't it?"

"Seem unfair? It is unfair."

"Let's not be too hasty. You are thinking too much in temporal terms, as though eternity is merely an extension of time. I think it comes again to the question of free will. If God were to give some of those in hell millions of chances to repent, I think he knows better than we that they would reject his offer again and again. You make hell out to be a prison, when in reality it is a choice. God respects the choice. Thy will be done, says he. Like the dwarfs at the end of my book *The Last Battle*, those who reject God refuse to see heaven. They are imprisoned by their own shortsighted minds."

"I don't think your answer is satisfactory, but I will give it some thought. Now, what about annihilation? Instead of putting individuals in hell—or respecting their choice, as you might put it—why not simply destroy them?"

"There was a time when I might have agreed with that perspective, but not anymore. The Bible does not teach annihilation. Christ said, in the Gospel of Saint Matthew, 'Depart from me, ye cursed, into everlasting fire,' not temporary fire. 'These shall go away into everlasting punishment,' he added, not temporary punishment. Granted, I am no theologian, but from what I gather from a plain reading of the biblical text, hell is forever. Therefore, annihilation is ruled out. I'm afraid the choice for immortals remains heaven or hell."

I said nothing in reply. Hell still seemed to me a barbaric relic of ages past. Something used by preachers and parents as a scare tactic. But I could understand something of Jack's logic. If he really believed in the reliability of the New Testament, then it followed that he believed in the reliability of the words and actions of Christ therein. If Christ had indeed said such things about hell, then logically Jack had to believe them.

"And what of heaven?" I asked, after a short pause in our conversation.

"It is our true country—where we should be, as God intends." Jack sipped more tea.

"But how do you know it is real? And this time, no appealing to the Bible."

"I don't think I have to in this case. The reality of heaven is inextricably tied to our earthly longings and desires—our joy, in my terms."

"You mentioned this at Little Lea. But I still don't see how longing makes the case for heaven."

"Oh, but it does. Every desire we experience on this earth has a means of fulfillment. When we are hungry, we eat. Sexual appetites have a means of satisfaction, with God's monogamous terms of marriage being the ideal solution. But what if there is a desire in me that nothing on this world seems to satisfy? What if I search for it my whole life—in travel, in women, in hobbies—and yet it continues to elude me? Does it not seem that the reason I have not satisfied this desire may be that I am destined for another world—my true country—where this desire will ultimately be satisfied? I think so."

"That seems an oversimplification."

"Oh? Both Augustine and Pascal understood the true meaning of our longings. Augustine said it in his famous quotation from *Confessions*, that our hearts find no peace until they rest in God. Pascal wrote that individuals seek to fill an emptiness in their lives with happiness, but no matter how hard they try, they cannot satisfy this desire, 'since this infinite abyss can be filled only with an infinite and immutable object; in other words by God himself.' Our true country—heaven, based on the reality of God—is where this longing will be fulfilled. Look to earth and you are searching in the wrong place. Look to heaven and your deepest desire, which nothing in this world can satisfy, will provide the answer."

"And what if someone does not have this desire—this longing?"

"Everyone does, but not all admit it or realize it. They spend their lives restless, knowing deep down inside that things are not quite right. They fill their time with distractions of various sorts, never stopping long enough to examine themselves. And here I find myself in agreement with Socrates—'The unexamined life is not worth living.'"

"On that we can agree, but I don't agree with your conclusions."

"Tom, you still have some time to make your choice. Life is a great story. This world—this life—is merely a shadow of what God wants for each of us. His great story goes on throughout eternity, always getting better and better. Make the right choice, Tom, and enter your true country. Follow the evidence, wherever it leads. And now it is time for me to move on."

We left the common room, as I followed Jack through the Kilns. He stopped at the doorway to a bedroom. I quickly glanced around. Two full bookshelves were against one wall. In front of the shelves was a reading chair. The bed, much to my surprise, was occupied by Jack, but he looked sickly and old. I turned to my right and saw another Jack, presumably the Jack who I'd spent the last several hours talking with, but now he appeared transparent, as though he were fading. He looked at himself on the bed, then at me.

"I was ready to go, you know," the Jack standing next to me said quietly. "I told Warnie that I believed I had done all that I wanted to do on this earth.

"Do I look that bad?" he asked, noticing the concerned expression on my face as I looked at the bedridden Jack, who did not seem to be able to see us. I did not answer because he did indeed look bad.

"Yes, I do look rather weary, don't I? I am near death, you know. The day began so—" he faltered, "so normally. After breakfast Warnie brought the letters and we went through them. I remember one contained an invitation for me to lecture. I wanted to do it, but knew my body could not withstand it. I asked Warnie to write a polite letter declining the invitation."

He spoke distantly, to no one in particular.

"After letters I worked on a crossword puzzle. We ate lunch then I took a nap in a chair. When I awoke, Warnie asked if I wouldn't be more comfortable in bed. I agreed. Later he brought me tea. It was the last time I spoke to him. I was ready to go; as Shakespeare's *King Lear* records, 'Men must endure their going hence.'"

A quiet knock at the door, which I had closed after we entered the room, interrupted us.

"Jack? Jack, I have your tea."

Warren opened the door, apparently unable to see us now, and seemed to walk through us. He set the tea down on the nightstand. I held up a hand in front of my face and noticed the transparency had returned.

"Thank you, Warnie," said the bedridden Jack.

"You look drowsy," Warnie told him.

"I am, but it will pass, I'm sure."

"Right then. Let me know if you need anything."

"Thank you, Warnie."

Warren left, quietly closing the door behind him.

"You are dying?" I asked.

"Yes. Everyone is, you know. You, too, Tom." He looked at me seriously and continued, "We've had some fruitful discussions. You have a sharp mind, but a stubborn will. Don't wait too long to make your choice. Follow the evidence."

"I need to be sure," I began. "I don't want to make the wrong choice."

"But you are living as though you have already chosen."

"I suppose you're right," I answered. Just then I noticed a calendar on the wall. November 22, 1963. "Hey, Jack," I said, pointing to the calendar, "wasn't that the day Kennedy was assassinated—"

Jack looked at me sadly, unresponsive to my distraction. "It's time for me to go, Tom." He walked over to the bed and joined the bedridden Jack, who was now the only Jack in the room, still looking ill and tired. He seemed to be trying to get up, but as he tried, he fell to the floor with a crash. I quickly knelt beside him, supporting his neck with one arm.

"Jack? Jack! Warnie!" I yelled.

"It's all right, Tom," whispered Jack as he looked up at me. "You are the one I am worried about." He coughed. "There is still hope for you, Tom. While you live, there is still hope. For me, this is the way the world ends." His eyes suddenly filled with mirth.

"What is it?"

"Warnie's toy garden. No, it's not a garden," said Jack, feebly. "It is him. My Lord, I believe . . ." He said no more.

I heard footsteps approaching. I gently let Jack's head rest on the floor and moved away. Warren entered, still not seeing me, a look of shock spreading across his face. He knelt next to Jack.

"Jack. Jack? No . . . No . . . not like this, not now." Warren held his brother, held the now lifeless body of C. S. Lewis, and wept. Tears were running down my face too. I couldn't bear to look, so I covered my eyes.

Somehow I stumbled out of the room. When I stopped, I saw the wardrobe before me, door open. Peering through it, I could just make out my hospital room. Several people were standing around my bed. I carefully stepped into the wardrobe, then through it.

Epilogue

Wherein I return to my proper place and resume my journey.

I stood still for a moment, my hands still covering my face. The wardrobe vanished. Slowly, I lowered my hands and saw the ugly vinyl chair where I had first seen Jack. I was back in my hospital room, that was certain, but a strange sight was before me.

I saw several medical personnel, busily gathered around my bed. Assuming they had gathered because of concern regarding my absence I called out to them.

"I'm here, I'm here! I've come back. I'm all right!"

But they did not respond. Instead, they continued speaking to one another in urgent tones. I heard a rapid beeping noise that soon turned into a steady tone.

"Should I call it, doctor?" a nurse asked.

"No, let's try once more," replied a man I did not recognize.

"It's all right. I've come back!" I called to them. Again, no response. I took a few steps closer. To my horror, I saw myself in the bed, looking pale and exhausted. The doctor applied the paddles of the defibrillator to my chest and I saw my body heave upwards, still lifeless, the steady tone continuing. I held my hand up to look at it and noticed that it was still transparent.

Confusion overwhelmed me. Jack had talked sense, but I wasn't ready to give in. I wasn't ready to yield or admit defeat in my quest for truth. It would be so easy to let go. But what then? What if Jack was right and I was wrong? If God really did exist and did in fact do what Jack believed him to have done through Christ, well then, that deserved more thought, didn't it? I would not yield to death—not yet.

The doctor looked at his watch, "Time of death—"

But I wasn't dead! I approached my body and entered it, as I had seen Jack do with his body. I opened my eyes, gasped for breath, once again felt the pain of my decaying body and heard the steady tone begin to beep. A flurry of more attention from the doctor and nurses followed.

Eventually they let me be, advising me to get some much needed rest. But I couldn't sleep. Not after my talks with Jack. Did it all really happen, or was my ailing mind just playing tricks on me as I approached death?

After a few minutes a nurse came back to check on me. I remembered her. She had been particularly helpful in getting me settled some weeks before, despite providing me with pink slippers.

"Now, Mr. Clerk, you should be getting some rest, you know." She smiled.

"Yes, it's just that I have a lot on my mind," I said, my voice noticeably weak, the pain in my body causing me to wince.

"Well, considering you just cheated death, I can't imagine! There's hope, you know, Mr. Clerk. There's always hope." She walked to the window and opened the curtains wide. "Well, look at that, the storm has passed."

"And there's the sun—dawn is coming." She gestured to the window, smiled, turned and left.

I glanced at my food tray, my copy of *Mere Christianity* still upon it. When Jack asked me where I got it, when we first met, I had hesitated, not knowing how much to reveal to a stranger. I wish I'd had a chance to tell Jack that my wife—my ex-wife, rather—gave it to me. She had changed, that much I knew, but how much of her change was based on wishful thinking and how much, if any, was based on the existence of God?

"Follow the evidence, wherever it leads," Jack had said. That seemed like good advice. Maybe it was time to give the book another chance . . . maybe it was time to give Jack another chance. I picked it up and began to read.

Appendix A

Where Does Lewis Say That?

This appendix serves as a broad cross-reference to some of the main ideas and arguments discussed in each chapter. Reference to the primary works of Lewis, generally where ideas are developed in depth, are listed, as are useful secondary sources. These references are by no means exhaustive. Lewis often wrote about an idea in bits and pieces throughout his works. Such recurring themes include his concepts of desire and joy, his insights on imagination and more. Secondary works on Lewis are too numerous to list exhaustively. Readers interested in seeking more detailed information on a particular theme or topic may consult one of the many reference works listed in the acknowledgments and bibliography, where I have listed resources that were most valuable in my research.

Chapter 1: Surprised by C. S. Lewis
Mere Christianity and *The Lion, the Witch, and the Wardrobe* are mentioned in the chapter. For those new to the works of Lewis, the former work remains one of the best introductory resources.

Chapter 2: We Visit Jack's Childhood Home
An account of the incident involving Jack and Warnie digging for a pot

of gold is found in *Jack* by George Sayer. The concept of desire, longing and *Sehnsucht* are found in numerous places in the writings of Lewis. The primary sources consulted for this chapter include *Surprised by Joy* and *Mere Christianity*. Also see Peter J. Kreeft, "C. S. Lewis's Argument from Desire," in *G. K. Chesterton and C. S. Lewis: The Riddle of Joy*, ed. Michael Macdonald and Andrew Tadie. For more on Lewis's mother and father see *Surprised by Joy* and the Lewis biographies mentioned in the acknowledgments. Images of Little Lea are found, among other places, in *C. S. Lewis: Images of His World* and *Through Joy and Beyond.*

Chapter 3: Atheism and a Man I Can Relate To

For more on Lewis's conversion see Lewis's *Surprised by Joy* and *The Pilgrim's Regress*. David Downing does a fine job of tracing the conversion in *The Most Reluctant Convert*. George Sayer includes a chapter on Lewis's conversion in *Jack*, as do other biographers such as Alan Jacobs, Douglas Gresham, and Walter Hooper and Roger Lancelyn Green. For more on Lewis's views on education see *Irrigating Deserts* by Joel Heck. There is only one known photograph of W. T. Kirkpatrick, supposedly taken by Warren Lewis in 1920. It is reprinted in *Through Joy and Beyond* and, more recently, in *The Most Reluctant Convert*. For more on the question of logic and its relevance in relation to comprehending the reality of God and Christian truth see *Systematic Theology*, volume 1, by Norman Geisler. The nonsense words *bluspels* and *flalansferes* allude to an essay by Lewis, "Bluspels and Flalansferes," in *Selected Literary Essays* and *Rehabilitations and Other Essays.*

Chapter 4: Evil in the Trenches

On Lewis and the intellectual problem of evil see Lewis's *The Problem of Pain* and his short essay "Evil and God" in *God in the Dock*. For Lewis's views on pacifism see, "Why I Am Not a Pacifist," in *The Weight of Glory and Other Ad-*

dresses. Some of *The Screwtape Letters* also address the question of war, such as Letter V. Secondary sources on the problem of evil include *The Roots of Evil* by Norman Geisler, *C. S. Lewis's Case for Christ* by Art Lindsley, and the chapter "Peace and War" in my book *The Lion, the Witch, and the Bible* (reissued as *The Heart of Narnia*). Douglas Gresham recounts some of Lewis's experiences in World War I in *Lenten Lands.* The Lewis lecture "Learning in War Time," in *The Weight of Glory and Other Addresses,* may also be of interest. For a summary of Lewis's views on war see *Mere Theology* by Will Vaus, chapter 17.

Chapter 5: Can Ideas Destroy Humanity?

For primary source material see *The Abolition of Man* and *That Hideous Strength.* Lewis also touches upon these themes, though not as in-depth, in *The Magician's Nephew,* specifically via the characters of Jadis and Andrew. On Lewis's conversion to theism, as well as his important talk with Tolkien and Dyson, see *Surprised by Joy* and the many biographies of Lewis mentioned in the acknowledgments. For insightful commentary on *The Abolition of Man* see *C. S. Lewis for the Third Millennium: Six Essays on "The Abolition of Man"* by Peter Kreeft. For Lewis on animal cruelty and experimentation see *The Problem of Pain,* chapter 9, and "Vivisection" in *God in the Dock.*

Chapter 6: Conversion on a Motorbike

On Lewis's Christian conversion, and his conversion process, see Lewis's *Surprised by Joy* and *The Pilgrim's Regress,* particularly Lewis's "Afterword to the Third Edition." Secondary sources include *The Most Reluctant Convert* by David Downing, *The Narnian* by Alan Jacobs, *Jack* by George Sayer, and *Jack's Life* by Douglas Gresham. Lewis's ideas on conversion are scattered throughout his works. The Kilns is owned by the C. S. Lewis Foundation of Redlands, California. The Foundation has restored the home to its period appearance. The brick kilns, however, were demolished in 1968.

Chapter 7: A Mere Christian on the Air

For more on C. S. Lewis's relationship with the BBC see *C. S. Lewis in a Time of War* by Justin Phillips. For more on Lewis's arguments from morality and the argument from Christ see *Mere Christianity*, Books I and II. Also see "The Poison of Subjectivism" in *Christian Reflections*. The appendix to *The Abolition of Man* contains Lewis's evidence for natural law as found in various cultures and religions, all pointing to the same overarching standard of morality (Lewis's primary resource in support of this research was the *Encyclopaedia of Religion and Ethics*, edited by James Hastings). Lewis encountered the argument for Christ in *The Everlasting Man* by G. K. Chesterton. A version of the argument can be traced to *Demonstratio Evangelica (The Proof of the Gospel)*, book 3, chapter 5, by Eusebius of Caesarea (4th century). The argument was popularized by Josh McDowell in *More Than a Carpenter*. More recently it has been taken up at a popular level by Kenneth Samples in *Without a Doubt*, chapter 8, and by Stephen T. Davis in the essay "Was Jesus Mad, Bad, or God?" in *The Incarnation*. Peter Kreeft and Ronald Tacelli also address the argument in *Handbook of Christian Apologetics*, pp. 161-71. The reasoning behind the argument appears in *The Lion, the Witch, and the Wardrobe* when Professor Kirke suggests what the logical options are in the case of Lucy and her story of visiting another world. Regarding her alleged journey to Narnia via a wardrobe, the professor suggests Lucy is either telling the truth, deliberately lying or she is insane. A cogent summary of Lewis's argument from morality is found under the entry "Lewis, C. S." in *Baker Encyclopedia of Christian Apologetics* by Norman Geisler.

Chapter 8: Friends at the Pub

For more on the Inklings see *The Inklings* by Humphrey Carpenter and *The Inklings Handbook* by Colin Duriez and David Porter. On a wall in the Eagle and Child is a plaque with the following inscription upon it: "C. S. Lewis, his brother, W. H. Lewis, J. R. R. Tolkien, Charles Williams and other friends met every Tuesday morning between the years 1939–1962 in the back room of this their favourite pub. These men, popularly known as the 'Inklings,' met here to drink Beer and to discuss, among other things, the books they were writing."

See Lewis's *The Four Loves* for his insights on friendship. For insights on Lewis's view of truth see *Testing Christianity's Truth Claims*, pp. 331-39 by Gordon Lewis. For Lewis's insights on the concept of the inner ring see his essay "The Inner Ring" in *The Weight of Glory and Other Addresses*. The most overt references to the inner ring in Lewis's fiction are found in *That Hideous Strength*, as Mark Studdock desires to be a member of the inner ring of the N.I.C.E. For more on Lewis's argument from reason see chapter 3 of *Miracles* and *C. S. Lewis's Dangerous Idea* by Victor Reppert. For a more academic defense of the argument from reason by Reppert, including opposing views, see "Symposium on the Argument from Reason," *Philosophia Christi* 5, no. 1 (2003): 9-89.

Chapter 9: Mrs. Lewis and the Meaning of Grief

See Lewis's *A Grief Observed*, *The Four Loves* and *Mere Christianity*, Book III, chapters 5 and 6. For more on Lewis's relationship with Joy Gresham see *Lenten Lands* by Douglas Gresham, *And God Came In* by Lyle Dorsett (retitled *Joy and C. S. Lewis*), and *Jack* by George Sayer. For insights on Lewis's views of sex and love see *The Question of God*, chapters 6 and 7, by Armand Nicholi. Film adaptations of the story of Jack and Joy include the BBC production of *Through the Shadowlands*, starring Joss Ackland as Lewis, and the Hollywood production *Shadowlands*, starring Anthony Hopkins as Lewis. Both films have their flaws, with the BBC production generally being the more accurate of the two.

Chapter 10: Devil in the Gray Town

The ideas in this chapter are primarily my own. However, *The Great Divorce* provided inspiration for the setting, while *The Screwtape Letters* offered starting points for Tom's dialogue with Flubgose. In agreement with biblical revelation, Lewis believed in a literal devil, demons and angels. For further insights on Lewis's views of angels and demons, particularly in reference to Milton's *Paradise Lost*, see his *Preface to Paradise Lost*. For commentary on Lewis's depiction of the demonic in *The Screwtape Letters* see my book *Inside the Screwtape Letters*. Lewis also offers his insights on angelology in his Ransom trilogy *(Out of the Silent Planet, Perelandra* and *That Hideous Strength)*. For insightful commentary on the trilogy see *Planets in Peril* by David Downing. For more insights from the devil Flubgose, this time on prayer, see my article "Infernal Memorandum" in the November/December 2007 issue of *Pray!* magazine.

Chapter 11: Narnia and the World of Imagination

Imagination was a key theme in Lewis's writings and life. Helpful starting points on this topic include Lewis's *An Experiment in Criticism,* "On Stories" in *Of Other Worlds, Imagination and the Arts in C. S. Lewis* by Peter Schakel, and "Lewis, Truth, and Imagination" by Owen Barfield in *Owen Barfield on C. S. Lewis.* For balanced views of Christianity and imagination see *The Liberated Imagination* by Leland Ryken and *The Christian Imagination,* edited by Leland Ryken. Although it is not discussed in the chapter, Lewis's *Till We Have Faces* is perhaps his greatest imaginative literary work. For insightful commentary on this book see *Reason and Imagination in C. S. Lewis* by Peter Schakel. A summary of Lewis's ideas on imagination is found in Hooper's *C. S. Lewis: Companion & Guide,* pp. 564-74.

Chapter 12: Immortality, Hell and the Great Story

Lewis wrote a great deal on immortality, heaven and hell. See, for instance, specific chapters on heaven and hell in *The Problem of Pain*. See also his sermon "The Weight of Glory" in *The Weight of Glory and Other Addresses*, sections on longing and joy in *Surprised by Joy*, and portions of *Mere Christianity*. Lewis explored heaven and hell imaginatively in *The Great Divorce*, *The Last Battle* (heaven) and *The Screwtape Letters* (hell). For secondary sources on Lewis's views on these topics see *Beyond the Shadowlands: C. S. Lewis on Heaven and Hell* by Wayne Martindale and *Mere Theology* by Will Vaus, chapter 24. The quotation "Follow the evidence, wherever it leads" is a statement made by former atheist Anthony Flew, based on Plato's Socrates.

Appendix B

Who's Who?

While characters are described to varying degrees within the pages of
Conversations with C. S. Lewis, this appendix serves the purpose of
providing a quick reference to people featured in the book, not only as
characters but, in some cases, individuals mentioned. More information on these individuals is readily available in a number of works,
including *C. S. Lewis: Companion and Guide* by Walter Hooper, *The C. S.
Lewis Readers' Encyclopedia, The C. S. Lewis Encyclopedia,* biographical profiles
in *The Collected Letters of C. S. Lewis* and other sources. Some of the more
prominent individuals in this appendix have entire books written just
about them (for instance, Joy Gresham, J. R. R. Tolkien and Charles
Williams).

Peter William Bide (1912–2003). A former student of Lewis, Reverend
Bide agreed to perform the religious marriage ceremony (March 21,
1957) for Lewis and Joy Davidman despite lacking approval and author-
ity to do so from the Anglican Bishop of Oxford. At Lewis's request Bide
prayed for healing for Joy, which resulted in what doctors considered a
miraculous recovery. For a firsthand account of Bide's role in the marriage
ceremony and Joy Gresham's healing see *C. S. Lewis: Companion and Guide* by
Walter Hooper, pp. 633-35.

Henry Victor Dyson (1896–1975). Known as Hugo, Dyson was introduced to Lewis by a mutual friend, Neville Coghill, in 1930. First a lecturer and tutor at the University of Reading (1921–1945) and later a fellow and tutor at Merton College, Oxford (1945–1963), Dyson was also a member of the Inklings. Along with J. R. R. Tolkien, Dyson had a significant influence on Lewis's conversion to Christianity. Lewis dedicated *Rehabilitations and Other Essays* to Dyson, also mentioning Dyson's "untiring intellect" in the preface to *The Allegory of Love.*

Lizzie Endicott. As nursemaid to the Lewis brothers, Lizzie Endicott told the boys Irish folk stories. One day, after the boys had bathed and were taking their time drying themselves, Endicott said she would strike their "piggie-bottoms," resulting in the boys' coming up with lifelong nicknames for themselves: Archpiggiebotham (APB) for Warren Lewis and Smallpiggiebotham (SPB) for C. S. Lewis. While the character of the nurse in *Prince Caspian* may or may not be patterned after Endicott, the fact that she told stories to Caspian is reminiscent of Lewis's recollections of Endicott as found in *Surprised by Joy.*

J. B. S. Haldane (1892–1964). John Burdon Sanderson Haldane, quoted by Lewis in *Miracles* (Haldane's *Possible Worlds and Other Essays*) in reference to the argument from reason, and described by Walter Hooper as "a well-known biochemist, biologist and Marxist . . . Haldane hated Christianity" (Hooper, *C. S. Lewis: Companion & Guide,* 206). Haldane interpreted Lewis's Ransom trilogy as opposing science, leading Lewis to write "A Reply to Professor Haldane," compiled in *Of Other Worlds.*

William Thompson Kirkpatrick (1848–1921). Former headmaster of Lurgan College, Northern Ireland, Kirkpatrick tutored Lewis from 1914 to 1917. A former Presbyterian turned atheist, Kirkpatrick was admired by Lewis for his superb logic. Kirkpatrick was known by many nicknames, including "The Great Knock." Lewis patterned, in part, at least two fictional characters after him. These include Professor Digory

Kirke in the Narnia books, primarily *The Lion, the Witch, and the Wardrobe,*
The Magician's Nephew, and *The Last Battle,* and MacPhee in *That Hideous*
Strength. Under Kirkpatrick's tutelage, Lewis studied various languages,
classical literature and other subjects in preparation for college entrance
examinations. Distinct conversational mannerisms attributed to Kirkpatrick, as found in chapter 3—such as "I hear you," "Excuse" and
"Stop"—are found in Lewis's *Surprised by Joy.*

   Albert James Lewis (1863–1929). Lewis's father, Albert, served as a solicitor (lawyer) from 1889–1928. He died of cancer in 1929. Born in
Cork, Ireland, Albert married Florence Augusta Hamilton in 1894. In
1905 the family moved to Little Lea.

   Florence Augusta Hamilton Lewis (1862–1908). Irish-born Florence
("Flora") married Albert Lewis in 1894. She held degrees in logic and
mathematics from Queen's University. She died of cancer in 1908 in
Lewis's childhood home, Little Lea.

   Helen Joy Davidman Gresham Lewis (1915–1960). Born in New York and
raised in the Bronx, Joy Gresham first came to know Lewis via correspondence. A child of Jewish immigrants (her father from Poland, her mother
from Ukraine), Joy declared herself an atheist at an early age. Prior to her
conversion to Christianity, she was also a Marxist. In 1942 she married
William Lindsay Gresham. They had two children, David (b. 1942) and
Douglas (b. 1945). Despite the fact that William, too, claimed conversion
to Christianity, he expressed interest in various occult practices and alternative religions such as Scientology. Joy first met Lewis in 1952 when she
visited England, where she later moved in 1953. She divorced William in
1954. In 1956 she was diagnosed with cancer. Lewis wrote *A Grief Ob-*
served under the pseudonym N. W. Clerk in response to her death ("N. W."
stood for "Nat Whilk," meaning "I know not whom" in Anglo-Saxon,
while "clerk" meant "scholar"). Joy authored several poems, some novels

and *Smoke on the Mountain* (1953), a book about the Ten Commandments with a preface by Lewis.

Warren Hamilton Lewis (1895–1973). Older brother to Lewis, Warren ("Warnie") served in World War I and II. Warren was also tutored by W. T. Kirkpatrick. While not as prolific or well-known an author as his brother, Warren authored six books on seventeenth-century France, including *The Splendid Century* and *The Sunset of the Splendid Century.* Warren also compiled the "Lewis papers"—a vast collection of correspondence and other family papers. His lengthy biography of C. S. Lewis (abbreviated for publication in *Letters of C. S. Lewis*), which remains unpublished in its unabridged form, is part of the Marion E. Wade Center of Wheaton College.

Edward Francis Courtenay Moore (1898–1918). "Paddy" Moore, mentioned in passing in chapter 4, was Jack's roommate in Keble College, Oxford, 1917, during their time in the Officers' Training Corps. Knowing that they would both serve in the Great War, they made a pact that if one of them did not survive, the other would look after the family of the deceased. First reported missing, Paddy was later confirmed dead—killed in action. After the war Lewis cared for Paddy's sister, Maureen (1906–1997), and mother, Janie King Moore (1872–1951).

Frederick William Calcutt Paxford (1898–1979). Paxford was Lewis's handyman at the Kilns from 1930 until Lewis's death in 1963. Born the same year as Lewis, Paxford died in 1979 in his home in Churchill. His reminiscences about Lewis may be found in *We Remember C. S. Lewis,* edited by David Graham, and in *The Canadian C. S. Lewis Journal* (No. 55, Summer 1986). By all accounts, Paxford was a perpetually gloomy sort, always pointing out the negative aspects of life, yet seemingly remaining internally carefree. Lewis patterned a character in *The Silver Chair,* Puddleglum the Marsh-wiggle, after Paxford.

John Ronald Reuel Tolkien (1892–1973). Best known as the author of *The*

Hobbit and *The Lord of the Rings,* South African-born J. R. R. Tolkien was a close friend to C. S. Lewis and a member of the Inklings. Professionally, Tolkien served at Oxford as professor of Anglo-Saxon and, later, of English language and literature. A Roman Catholic, Tolkien remained disappointed that Lewis did not join the Church. He did not care for the Narnia stories, primarily because of the mixing of various mythologies—something Tolkien frowned on. Lewis dedicated *The Screwtape Letters* to Tolkien.

James William Welch (1900–1967). Director of religious broadcasting for the BBC from 1939–1942, Welch had read *The Problem of Pain* and, as a result, contacted Lewis in 1941 regarding some potential broadcast talks. Like Lewis, Welch was Anglican, but unlike Lewis, Welch was an ordained minister. For more on the relationship between Lewis and the BBC, see *C. S. Lewis in a Time of War* by Justin Phillips.

Charles Walter Stansby Williams (1886–1945). Author Charles Williams is perhaps best remembered for what T. S. Eliot referred to as "supernatural thrillers," including *War in Heaven.* Lewis in particular appreciated *The Place of the Lion.* The influence of Williams on Lewis is clearly evident in *That Hideous Strength,* the only novel in Lewis's space trilogy set entirely on earth, but with supernatural elements playing a vital role in events both for good and evil. Williams served as an editor with Oxford University Press until his death in 1945. Although Williams was Anglican, he dabbled in the occult religion known as Rosicrucianism.

Bibliography

Barfield, Owen. *Owen Barfield on C. S. Lewis*. Middletown, Conn.: Wesleyan University Press, 1990.

Carpenter, Humphrey. *The Inklings*. Boston: Houghton Mifflin, 1979.

Como, James T., ed. *Remembering C. S. Lewis: Recollections of Those Who Knew Him*. San Francisco: Ignatius Press, 2005.

Coren, Michael. *The Man Who Created Narnia*. Grand Rapids: Eerdmans, 1994.

Davidman, Joy. *Smoke on the Mountain*. Philadelphia: Westminster Press, 1953.

Davis, Stephen T., Daniel Kendall and Gerald O'Collins, eds. *The Incarnation*. New York: Oxford University Press, 2002.

Dorsett, Lyle. *And God Came In*. Wheaton, Ill.: Good News Publishers, 1991.

Downing, David. *The Most Reluctant Convert*. Downers Grove, Ill.: InterVarsity Press, 2002.

—————. *Planets in Peril: A Critical Study of C. S. Lewis's Ransom Trilogy*. Amherst: University of Massachusetts Press, 1995.

Duncan, John Ryan. *The Magic Never Ends: An Oral History of the Life and Work of C. S. Lewis*. Nashville: W Publishing Group, 2001.

Duriez, Colin. *The C. S. Lewis Encyclopedia*. Wheaton, Ill.: Crossway, 2000.

Duriez, Colin, and David Porter. *The Inklings Handbook*. Atlanta: Chalice, 2001.

Frazer, James. *The Golden Bough: A Study in Magic and Religion* (abridged edition). Ware, U.K.: Wordsworth Reference, 1993.

Geisler, Norman. *Baker Encyclopedia of Christian Apologetics.* Grand Rapids: Baker, 1999.

————. *The Roots of Evil.* Eugene, Ore.: Wipf and Stock, 2002.

————. *Systematic Theology.* Vol. I, *Introduction/Bible.* Minneapolis: Bethany House, 2002.

Geisler, Norman, Alex McFarland, and Robert Velarde. *10 Questions and Answers on Atheism and Agnosticism.* Torrance, Cal.: Rose, 2007.

Gilbert, Douglas R., and Clyde S. Kilby. *C. S. Lewis: Images of His World.* Grand Rapids: Eerdmans, 2005.

Graham, David, ed. *We Remember C. S. Lewis.* Nashville: Broadman & Holman, 2001.

Green, Roger Lancelyn, and Walter Hooper. *C. S. Lewis: A Biography.* London: HarperCollins, 2002.

Gresham, Douglas. *Jack's Life.* Nashville: Broadman & Holman, 2005.

————. *Lenten Lands.* New York: Macmillan, 1988.

Heck, Joel. *Irrigating Deserts: C. S. Lewis on Education.* St. Louis: Concordia Publishing House, 2005.

Hooper, Walter, ed. *The Collected Letters of C. S. Lewis, Vol. I: Family Letters 1905–1931.* San Francisco: HarperSanFrancisco, 2004.

————. *The Collected Letters of C. S. Lewis, Vol. II: Books, Broadcasts, and the War 1931–1949.* San Francisco: HarperSanFrancisco, 2004.

————. *The Collected Letters of C. S. Lewis, Vol. III: Narnia, Cambridge, and Joy 1950–1963.* San Francisco: HarperSanFrancisco, 2007.

————. *C. S. Lewis: Companion & Guide.* San Francisco: HarperSanFrancisco, 1996.

————. *Through Joy and Beyond.* New York: Macmillan, 1982.

Jacobs, Alan. *The Narnian.* San Francisco: HarperSanFrancisco, 2005.

Kreeft, Peter. *Between Heaven and Hell: A Dialog Somewhere Beyond Death with John F. Kennedy, C. S. Lewis, and Aldous Huxley.* Downers Grove, Ill.: InterVarsity Press, 1982.

————. *C. S. Lewis for the Third Millennium: Six Essays on "The Abolition of Man."* San Francisco: Ignatius Press, 1994.

Kreeft, Peter, and Ronald Tacelli. *Handbook of Christian Apologetics*. Downers Grove, Ill.: InterVarsity Press, 1994.

Lewis, C. S. *The Abolition of Man*. New York: Macmillan, 1978.

————. *The Allegory of Love*. New York: Oxford University Press, 1965.

————. *Christian Reflections*. Grand Rapids: Eerdmans, 1967.

————. *An Experiment in Criticism*. New York: Cambridge University Press, 1961.

————. *The Four Loves*. New York: Harcourt Brace, 1960.

————. *God in the Dock*. Grand Rapids: Eerdmans, 1970.

————. *The Great Divorce*. New York: Macmillan, 1946.

————. *A Grief Observed*. New York: Bantam, 1976.

————. *The Last Battle*. New York: Harper Trophy, 2000.

————. *Letters to Malcolm: Chiefly on Prayer*. New York: Harcourt, 1963.

————. *The Lion, the Witch, and the Wardrobe*. New York: Harper Trophy, 2000.

————. *The Magician's Nephew*. New York: Harper Trophy, 2000.

————. *Mere Christianity*. New York: Macmillan, 1952.

————. *Miracles*. New York: Macmillan, 1978.

————. *Of Other Worlds*. New York: Harcourt Brace, 1975.

————. *Out of the Silent Planet*. New York: Macmillan, 1965.

————. *Perelandra*. New York: Macmillan, 1965.

————. *The Pilgrim's Regress*. Grand Rapids: Eerdmans, 1992.

————. *A Preface to Paradise Lost*. New York: Oxford University Press, 1961.

————. *Prince Caspian*. New York: Harper Trophy, 2000.

————. *The Problem of Pain*. New York: Macmillan, 1962.

————. *Rehabilitations and Other Essays*. London: Oxford University Press, 1939.

————. *The Screwtape Letters*. New York: Macmillan, 1982.

————. *Selected Literary Essays*. Edited by Walter Hooper. Cambridge: Cambridge University Press, 1979.

————. *The Silver Chair*. New York: Harper Trophy, 2000.

————. *Spirits in Bondage*. San Diego: Harcourt Brace Jovanovich, 1984.

————. *Surprised by Joy*. New York: Harcourt Brace, 1956.

————. *That Hideous Strength*. New York: Macmillan, 1965.

————. *Till We Have Faces.* New York: Harcourt, 1956.

————. *The Weight of Glory and Other Addresses.* New York: Macmillan, 1980.

Lewis, Gordon. *Testing Christianity's Truth Claims.* New York: University Press of America, 1990.

Lewis, Warren. *Letters of C. S. Lewis, Revised and Enlarged Edition.* New York: Harcourt, 1993.

Lindsley, Art. *C. S. Lewis's Case for Christ.* Downers Grove, Ill.: InterVarsity Press, 2005.

Macdonald, Michael H., and Andrew A. Tadie, eds. *G. K. Chesterton and C. S. Lewis: The Riddle of Joy.* Grand Rapids: Eerdmans, 1989.

Martindale, Wayne. *Beyond the Shadowlands: C. S. Lewis on Heaven and Hell.* Wheaton, Ill.: Crossway, 2005.

McDowell, Josh. *More Than a Carpenter.* Wheaton, Ill.: Tyndale House, 1977.

Nicholi, Armand M. *The Question of God: C. S. Lewis and Sigmund Freud Debate God, Love, Sex, and the Meaning of Life.* New York: Free Press, 2002.

Phillips, Justin. *C. S. Lewis in a Time of War.* San Francisco: HarperSanFrancisco, 2002.

Reppert, Victor. *C. S. Lewis's Dangerous Idea: In Defense of the Argument from Reason.* Downers Grove, Ill.: InterVarsity Press, 2003.

Ryken, Leland. *The Liberated Imagination.* Colorado Springs: Waterbrook, 1989.

————, ed. *The Christian Imagination.* Colorado Springs: Waterbrook, 2002.

Samples, Kenneth. *Without a Doubt.* Grand Rapids: Baker, 2004.

Sayer, George. *Jack: A Life of C. S. Lewis.* Wheaton, Ill.: Crossway, 1994.

Schakel, Peter. *Imagination and the Arts in C. S. Lewis.* Columbia: University of Missouri Press, 2002.

————. *Reason and Imagination in C. S. Lewis: A Study of "Till We Have Faces."* Grand Rapids: Eerdmans, 1984.

Schultz, Jeffery D., and John G. West Jr., eds. *The C. S. Lewis Readers' Encyclopedia.* Grand Rapids: Zondervan, 1998.

Vaus, Will. *Mere Theology: A Guide to the Thought of C. S. Lewis.* Downers Grove, Ill.: InterVarsity Press, 2004.

Velarde, Robert. *Inside the Screwtape Letters.* Grand Rapids: Baker, 2008.

————. *The Lion, the Witch, and the Bible: Good and Evil in the Classic Tales of C. S. Lewis.* Colorado Springs: NavPress, 2005 (reprinted as *The Heart of Narnia,* 2008).

Acknowledgments

John Donne wrote, "No man is an island, entire of itself." Neither is a book. I owe a great debt of thanks not only to C. S. Lewis for producing such wonderful works, but to Lewis scholars past and present for providing a rich source of research material.

Although *Conversations with C. S. Lewis* is a work of creative fiction, it contains factual information about people, places and ideas (though the interpretation of ideas is another matter). My primary biographical sources included *Jack* by George Sayer, *Lenten Lands* and *Jack's Life* by Douglas Gresham, *C. S. Lewis: A Biography* by Roger Lancelyn Green and Walter Hooper, *The Narnian* by Alan Jacobs and *The Most Reluctant Convert* by David Downing. I also consulted a number of reference works in researching this book, but four stand out: *The C. S. Lewis Encyclopedia* by Colin Duriez, *The C. S. Lewis Readers' Encyclopedia* edited by Jeffrey Schultz and John West Jr., *Mere Theology* by Will Vaus and *C. S. Lewis: Companion and Guide* by Walter Hooper. Books containing various historical photographs helped me in creating the settings for *Conversations with C. S. Lewis*. These works included *Through Joy and Beyond* by Walter Hooper, *C. S. Lewis: Images of His World* by Douglas Gilbert and Clyde Kilby, *The Magic Never Ends* by John Ryan Duncan and *The Man Who Created Narnia* by Michael Coren. Edited by Walter Hooper, all three volumes of *The Collected Letters of C. S. Lewis* were also of great interest and inspiration. I am grateful to each of the above authors for providing ample research material.

Many thanks are also due to Peter Kreeft. His fine book *Between Heaven and Hell*, which features fictional conversations between C. S. Lewis, Aldous Huxley and John F. Kennedy, provided the initial inspiration for *Conversations with C. S. Lewis*.

I also found several films of help, particularly in reference to photographs and images of locations in the life of Lewis. These films included *The Magic Never Ends: The Life and Work of C. S. Lewis*, *C. S. Lewis: Beyond Narnia* and *C. S. Lewis: Dreamer of Narnia*.

I am also thankful to Andy Le Peau, Al Hsu and the rest of the gifted team at InterVarsity Press for helping make *Conversations with C. S. Lewis* a reality.

My fellow Linklings deserve a word of praise for their steadfast encouragement: Brian Elliott, William Mitchell, Rodger Pfingsten and Shana Schutte.

My wife, Candace, and my four children, Anthony, Vincent, Dante and Marcus, deserve an abundance of thanks for their love, patience and encouragement during my many sequestered hours working on the manuscript. My wife also deserves a word of praise for her speedy and insightful proofreading notations on an early draft of the manuscript.

Name Index

Subject Index

About the Author

A former atheist, Robert Velarde is author of *The Heart of Narnia: Wisdom, Virtue, and Life Lessons from the Classic Chronicles* (NavPress) and *Inside the Screwtape Letters* (Baker Book House). Robert is coauthor of *Examining Alternative Medicine* (InterVarsity Press) and *10 Questions and Answers on Atheism and Agnosticism* (Rose Publishing). He is a member of the Evangelical Theological Society, Evangelical Philosophical Society, the Society of Christian Philosophers and the International Society of Christian Apologetics. Robert studied philosophy of religion at Denver Seminary and is pursuing graduate studies in philosophy at Southern Evangelical Seminary. A classically trained pianist, he received his undergraduate degree in music from California State University, Long Beach, and has composed music for flute and piano inspired by scenes from the Chronicles of Narnia. Robert resides in Colorado Springs, Colorado, with his wife, four children, a feisty beagle and lots of books.

Visit his blog at http://robertvelarde.blogspot.com or contact him at conversationswithcslewis@gmail.com.